EMPTY NEST YEARS

How to Adult (Again) After Raising Kids — An Uplifting & Witty Guide to Reclaim Joy, Purpose, and Your New Exciting Chapter.

The information in this book is for inspiration and self-reflection.

Author: Natalie Huley

ISBN 978-83-977633-1-9

TABLE OF CONTENTS

For every woman
who has ever looked at her empty nest
and thought, "Now what?" May this be the
reminder that what comes next can be just
as full of laughter, freedom,
and unexpected adventures.

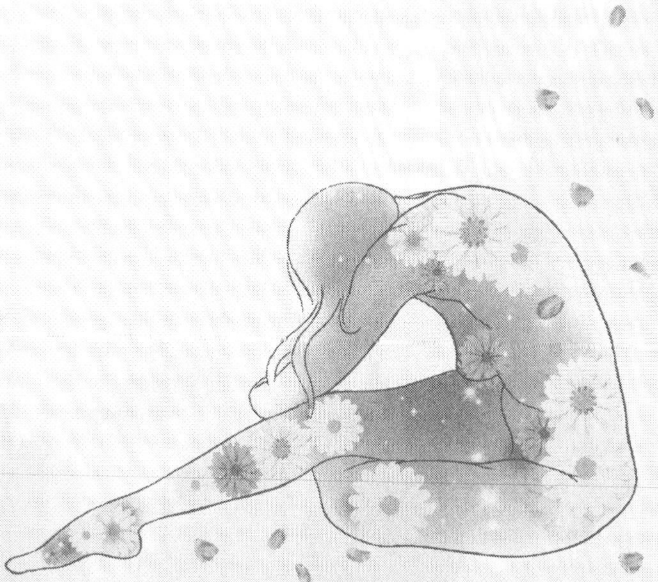

Introduction: The Life No One Prepared You For

Dear Woman standing at the start of her next chapter,

Your last child has just left for college, or perhaps turned twenty-five and finally moved out. Maybe you have reached that moment when they no longer need you for daily things: no more games to watch, no more school projects to rescue at the last minute, no more friends drama to solve. Suddenly, you find yourself sitting in a strangely quiet house, looking at a calendar that for the first time in decades is not filled with anyone else's appointments but your own, and you wonder: What do I do now?

If you have picked up this book, you are probably somewhere in the midst of what people call the "empty nest." Yet nobody explained that it is not only about the silence in your home but also about the profound questioning of who you are when you're no longer needed to be a full-time mother.

Perhaps you cried for the first week after your child left, feeling like a soldier who had just finished a twenty-year before and suddenly did not know how to live in peacetime. Perhaps it has been six months, and you still catch yourself standing in the kitchen at four in the afternoon, wondering why you are automatically planning dinner for four when you are alone. Or perhaps you were one of those women who expected to feel thrilled with freedom, only to discover that freedom can be unsettling when you no longer remember what you wanted before everything revolved around your children's needs.

What matters most right now is to know that everything you are feeling is normal. Missing being needed is normal.

Feeling lost without the daily structure that came with children is normal. Experiencing moments when you feel like a stranger in your own life is also normal. Panicking when you realize you do not know how to fill a Saturday morning without practice or games is entirely normal. And you are certainly not unusual if you did not immediately throw yourself into new hobbies and travel plans. You are simply a woman who, for years, defined yourself through what you did for others, and now you are faced with the task of discovering who you are when your efforts are directed toward yourself.

Although that might sound simple, in reality, it is a particularly challenging transition. Nobody ever prepared you for how disorienting an empty calendar feels after decades of managing the schedules of an entire family. Few people tell you that it may take a year or two before you begin to feel at home in this new role. And very few will warn you that everyone around you—whether your sister, your daughter, or your friends—may assume that you are now permanently available because you suddenly "have time."

This book will not tell you to be grateful for freedom or to treat this as the best time of your life. Instead, it will help you navigate the real, often messy process of discovering what your life can look like when it is no longer organized around your children. It will allow you to grieve what you have lost, because it is a loss, even if it is a necessary and ultimately good one. And it will invite you to rebuild your days slowly, at your own pace, without pressure to transform overnight, until you arrive at a life that is truly yours.

Most importantly, these pages will treat you as the capable, intelligent woman you are, someone going through a profound life change, not as a person in need of motivational slogans or simplistic solutions. I know that you may also be navigating the care of aging parents who require more attention, just as you imagined your responsibilities decreasing. Your finances may be tied up with tuition payments, mortgage obligations, and retirement planning rather than carefree European vacations. Your marriage may need rediscovery, as you relearn how to be a couple who talks about something other than family logistics. And your body and energy may not be the same as they were twenty years ago, when you last thought seriously about your own needs.

Yet I also know this: if you have raised children who are now capable of living independently, you already possess every skill necessary to build a fulfilling life for yourself.

The problem-solving, the time management, the conflict mediation, the creativity in moments of crisis, the infinite capacity for love and care—none of these abilities have disappeared. They are simply waiting for you to direct them toward your own goals.

This new chapter will take time and will require patience. There will be days filled with possibility and days filled with longing for the simplicity of a clearly defined role. Both are part of the process. What matters is that you are fully capable of shaping a life that brings not only efficiency but also joy.

You deserve that life, and it is waiting for you.

The chapters ahead are divided into three natural parts of the journey.

Part I

The Empty Nest Reality Check, explores the truth of what this transition feels like, why it is so challenging, why it often takes longer than expected, and why every one of your emotions makes perfect sense.

Part II

Rebuilding Your Nest (for One), will guide you to remember who you were before motherhood, to reclaim time for yourself, to reconnect with your body and style, and to learn how to say no to what drains you.

Part III

Flying Solo (and Loving It), will focus on reshaping your relationships on new terms, protecting your time from others' expectations, caring for your health as a priority, and consciously designing a future that reflects the woman you are becoming.

Are you ready? Your real life is waiting, and it has the potential to be richer, more authentic, and more deeply satisfying than you ever imagined.

With respect for this journey and admiration for the woman you already are,

Natalie Huley

PART I

The Empty Nest Reality Check

Chapter 1

The Day The House Went Quiet — When Silence Sounds Like A Scream

> *How wild it was, to let it be.*
>
> Cheryl Strayed

You stand in the kitchen with a mug of coffee in your hand, staring at the refrigerator where last year's soccer schedule still clings, curling at the edges. For twenty years, your mornings began in a rush of shouted reminders about missing socks, late alarms, and sandwiches hastily assembled before the school bus arrived. Now the coffee cools before you have even taken a sip, and the gift of time feels less like freedom and more like a weight pressing against your chest.

The silence of the house has a presence, heavy and unyielding. The kitchen table, once the command center of family life, has lost its sense of urgency. Here you once hovered over homework sheets late at night, comforted your daughter through her first heartbreak, and sketched birthday plans on scraps of paper while balancing the monthly budget. That same table now feels too large, its surface polished and waiting, almost formal, as if stripped of its purpose.

The house itself exhales differently. The echoes of footsteps on the stairs at dawn, the refrigerator door opening and slamming every few minutes, the music blasting from upstairs so loudly you feared the neighbors might complain—these sounds have all faded into memory.

Your friends insist you are lucky, that you now have the chance to do anything you want, and you nod with a smile because that is the expected response. Yet deep inside, you are confronted with a truth that unsettles you: you no longer know what you want. Your desires have been stored away like books in a cardboard box in the attic, packed carefully during the constant relocations of family life, forgotten and gathering dust.

You once imagined the luxury of going to the movies alone or reading a book without the inevitable interruption of "Mom, where's my charger?" You dreamed of taking a bath without the sound of knocking at the bathroom door. Now all of these possibilities lie within reach. Yet, they bring you no clarity, only a strange sense of disorientation, like a traveler who boards a long-anticipated flight and suddenly realizes she cannot remember why she wanted to visit that destination in the first place.

You wake in the morning and remain in bed, listening for the sounds that used to shape your days: cabinet doors banging, showers running, hurried footsteps on the stairs, the desperate cry of "I can't find my shirt!" Instead, there is only silence, a silence so profound that it feels as if every clock in the house has stopped ticking.

With pride and emptiness intertwined, the realization strikes again and again. They no longer live here. They have their apartments, their friends, their struggles, and they no longer need you to document or approve every small choice. This was the outcome you worked toward, the ultimate goal of parenthood, and yet its arrival feels disorienting, like a conductor standing alone onstage after the orchestra has finished playing, baton still raised in her hand. At the same time, the audience files out into the night.

The practicalities of the house reflect the absence. The refrigerator remains full because no one raids it between meals. The bathroom stays clean for more than a day. The laundry piles have vanished. The snacks you once purchased specifically for each child remain untouched. Convenience should bring relief, yet instead, the order feels sterile, as if life has drained from the rooms. You find yourself slipping into old patterns without noticing, reaching for the yogurt with cartoon characters or your son's favorite cookies, only to realize at the checkout that no one will eat them now.

At the grocery store, you stall in the cereal aisle, overwhelmed by choices that once required no thought. For decades, you bought the same boxes, one for him, another for her, and a healthy one that no one liked but that you felt obliged to bring home anyway. Now you cannot remember what you honestly prefer. Do you even like cereal? When was the last time you chose food because it pleased you rather than because it was nutritious, affordable, or convenient for someone else? After standing frozen far too long, you leave with nothing but milk and coffee, safe purchases that require no reflection on who you are.

In the evenings, the television remote becomes yours alone. For an hour, you revel in the rare pleasure of watching without compromise. Yet eventually you begin to miss the disagreements, the complaints, the playful negotiations, even the interruptions that once seemed endless. They were proof that you belonged to something larger, that your presence mattered. Freedom can feel cumbersome, like wearing a heavy coat on a sweltering summer day.

When the phone rings, your heart leaps, certain it must be one of them reaching out, but too often it is only a telemarketer. You hang up with a wave of disappointment that surprises you. Once you longed for peace, and now you would give almost anything to hear, “Mom, can you pause the movie for a second?”

A friend calls to check in. She still has teenagers at home and complains about the chaos, the noise, the constant demands. You murmur understandingly while biting back the urge to tell her to savor every moment. When she asks how you are adjusting, you hear yourself reply, “It’s wonderful, I’m finally catching up on all the books I never had time for.” The words slide out so easily you almost believe them yourself. The truth is more complicated. You have started three novels and abandoned them all by chapter two, not because they failed to interest you but because the habit of interruption is so deeply ingrained that you keep lifting your head, waiting for someone to need you.

Sometimes you reach for the photo albums you have stored on a shelf. You flip through images of the first days of school with oversized backpacks, birthday parties filled with sugar-high children, Halloween costumes sewn at midnight because nothing store-bought ever felt good enough. In every photograph you are present, sometimes visibly in the frame, occasionally invisible but evident in the care that shaped the scene. You were the director, the producer, the steady presence behind every milestone. Now the performance has ended, and you sit alone in the empty theater, wondering if anyone will remember how much of it depended on you.

What you miss is not only your children. What you miss most painfully is the certainty of who you were when your role was unquestioned. Without the daily identity of "mother," you find yourself struggling to answer the simplest of questions: Who are you now? The mirror shows a woman who looks before but also strangely unclaimed, like someone waiting for instructions that never arrive.

At its core, an empty nest is not only about the absence of children in the house but about the moment you come face-to-face with yourself after decades of living for others and realize how unfamiliar you have become. It is not merely about missing the people who once filled your house. It is about meeting yourself again after decades of neglect and realizing that you are almost strangers.

The woman who longed to become a mother is not the same as the woman who lived that role, and the one who succeeded in raising children is now being asked to discover what else she is capable of becoming. It is as if someone handed you an unfamiliar instrument and expected you to play, though you have forgotten how to read the notes.

Your story has not ended. It is unfolding in a new form, written on a blank page that belongs solely to you. There are no instructions for what comes next, no ready-made script for a woman whose children no longer define her. That absence can feel terrifying, but it also carries extraordinary freedom. The question is no longer whether you will manage—because you will—but rather who you will allow yourself to become. For the first time in decades, the choice belongs entirely to you.

Write down three things you loved before you became a mother. Do not overthink them, do not censor them, and do not tell yourself you are too old. Write them down. They are the first breadcrumbs on the path back to yourself.

Chapter 2

"So... Now What?"— Staring At 30 Years Of Leftover Life

> *Maybe the journey isn't so much about becoming anything. Maybe it's about un-becoming everything that isn't you*
>
> Paulo Coelho

It's two in the morning, and you're staring at the ceiling, your body restless against the sheets. The same question circles in your mind, persistent as a melody you can't quite. "Now what?" It's deceptively simple, yet heavy enough to feel like you've been handed a riddle in a language you've never learned.

For twenty years, your "now what" was crystal clear: make breakfast, drive to practice, help with math homework. Life was a constant reaction to other people's needs, every square on the calendar crammed with obligations, leaving no room to wonder about the meaning of it all.

And now? You finally have the freedom you longed for, and it feels a bit like coffee you forgot to sweeten.

Morning comes, and for the first time in years, you wake up on your own. Your body still remembers the rhythm of school hours, so your eyes open at seven, but there's no reason to get up. You lie in bed thinking, "I can do whatever I want." The problem is, you don't know what you want. This freedom of choice that sounded like a prize turns out to be the burden of decisions nobody prepared you for.

The first hour passes, scrolling through social media. You see photos of friends on vacation, at restaurants, and in yoga classes. Everyone looks happy and fulfilled. You look like someone who received a ticket to anywhere in the world but can't decide where they want to go.

You decide to leave the house because being cooped up only makes it worse. But where? The mall seems pointless when you don't need to buy anything for anyone. The park is full of mothers with small children, and you feel like an intruder in a world you just exited. Art gallery? Too pretentious. Gym? Too late for new resolutions.

You end up in a coffee shop, ordering a latte and pretending to read a book. Still, you're watching other people and wondering if they're also asking themselves, "Now what?" or if you're the only one stuck in this existential loop.

Behind you in line stands a woman about your age, talking on the phone about her retirement plans. You catch fragments: "travel," "hobbies," "finally time for myself." She sounds like someone who has it all figured out, who knows what she wants from life. You feel like a student who didn't prepare for an exam in a subject whose name you don't even know.

You return home empty-handed with an even emptier head. You stand in the hallway, wondering if this is what people mean when they talk about a midlife crisis. Is this the moment when you buy a red car or sign up for dance classes? But you don't want a red car. You don't know if you're going to dance. You don't know what you want.

The internet doesn't help. You type "what to do after kids leave" into the search engine and get thousands of articles about how to "discover your passion" and "live your best life." All the experts have ready-made lists: travel, learn new things, volunteer, exercise, meditate. It sounds like recipes written in a foreign language: technically comprehensible but impossible to apply in practice.

You sign up for a newsletter about "life after fifty" and receive an email titled "10 Ways to Find Yourself." You read it, hopefully, but every piece of advice seems written for someone else, someone who has more energy, more confidence, more everything.

The next day, you try to be spontaneous. You get in the car without a destination and drive ahead. You pass stores where you shopped for the family, schools where you sent your kids, and playgrounds where you spent hundreds of hours. It's like touring a museum of your own life: everything looks familiar, but you're just an observer, not a participant.

You stop at a bookstore because books have always been your escape. But standing between the shelves, you realize you don't know what kind of books you're looking for. For years, you read quickly, secretly, between obligations. Now you have time for long, complicated novels, but you reach for something light because you're not sure you can handle something demanding.

The clerk asks if she can help. "I'm looking for something for myself," you say, and she smiles and asks, "What genre do you like?" You stand there for a long moment because you realize you don't know the answer to that question.

What do you like? Not as a mom, not as a wife, not as a professional. What do you like about yourself?

You leave the bookstore with a gardening guide, though you've never had a garden, and an Italian cookbook, though the closest you've been to Italy was a family vacation five years ago. It's like buying clothes in a size you don't know, hoping they'll somehow fit.

At home, you sit with these books and feel like a fraud. Do you want to learn how to grow tomatoes? Or is this just another attempt to fill time with something that sounds sensible? You read about soil preparation and wonder if you're not accidentally trying to prepare soil for a new life without knowing what you want to plant in it.

This uncertainty starts to piss you off. You're an intelligent woman who organized the lives of several people simultaneously for years, who could coordinate school plays, birthdays, vacations, and countless other events. Why can't you coordinate your happiness?

Maybe because, despite all those years as the conductor of an orchestra, you never learned to play solo.

One evening, you sit down with a piece of paper and a pen. You write "What do I want to do?" at the top and stare at the blank page. After ten minutes, you have one word: "I don't know." It's not the answer you were looking for, but maybe it's the most honest thing you've written in months.

Maybe "I don't know" isn't it. It may be a starting point.

You begin writing other questions. What brought me joy before kids? When did I last laugh until tears came? What did I do when time seemed to disappear? What were my dreams before they became dreams about my children's futures?

The answers come slowly, like photos developing in a darkroom. You liked dancing in the kitchen when nobody was watching. You liked long conversations about everything and nothing. You liked planning things: not just for others, but for yourself. You enjoyed learning new things, even if they weren't "practical."

This question, "Now what?" begins to change. From pressure, it becomes curiosity. From a problem, it becomes exploration. You don't need to know immediately who you'll be for the next thirty years. Maybe it's enough to see what you want to try tomorrow.

Maybe the answer to "Now what?" isn't a grand life plan, but a series of small experiments. Perhaps it's not a question you answer once and for all, but a question that evolves with you.

Morning comes, and you wake up with a new idea. Instead of asking "Now what?", you'll start asking "What if...?" What if you sign up for lessons in a language you have always wanted to learn? What if you visit that museum you've passed a thousand times but never had time to enter? What if you start talking to strangers in coffee shops?

These aren't big life decisions. These are small steps toward discovering who you might be.

For the first time in months, instead of going to bed with the question "Now what?", you go to bed thinking "We'll see."

And that's the beginning of everything.

Write ten questions starting with "What if...?"

Not about things you should do, but about things you might want to try. Allow yourself to dream without limits.

Chapter 3

It's Okay To Feel Lost — Why This Phase Is More Challenging Than Anyone Admits (And Why You're Not Failing)

> *The truth will set you free, but first it will piss you off.*
>
> Gloria Steinem

The lies begin early, and they are everywhere. Your neighbor beams across the fence and says, "Oh, you must be so excited to have the house to yourself finally." The store clerk notices that you are buying everything in singles now and chirps, "Empty nest, huh? Bet you're loving all that freedom." Your sister calls to gush about how this is your moment to rediscover yourself and pursue your passions.

Meanwhile, you are standing in the cereal aisle staring at an entire wall of colorful boxes, realizing that you have absolutely no clue what kind of cereal you even like. For years, you bought granola for your health-conscious daughter, protein cereal for your athlete son, and oatmeal for the one who suddenly went vegan. You always ate whatever was left, usually standing at the counter while someone yelled that they couldn't find their car keys.

Society has built a mythology around every major life transition, and for women, it comes with a relentless script. Teenage rebellion is typical; their need for distance is a healthy development, and their leaving is the natural order of things. People tell you to be proud that you raised independent children. They expect you to celebrate your newfound freedom, as if the late-night conversations about heartbreak, the endless worry about their safety, and the sleepless nights waiting for the sound of the door unlocking were nothing more than a rehearsal for this supposed glorious liberation. Home renovation shows tell you to turn your teenager's bedroom into a stylish home office. At the same time, you stand in the doorway staring at empty walls where band posters once clung, walls that only weeks ago held the echoes of music at midnight, slammed doors, and whispered phone calls.

No one admits that you might miss the fights about cleaning their room, or that the silence in the house you begged for can feel overwhelming, or that freedom from constant worry can leave you strangely useless. The truth is that transitions often feel like bullshit. The empty nest is no exception, yet few people are willing to admit it openly, because the world prefers stories of reinvention and glow-ups rather than grief. Your coworker who went through this five years ago looked at you with sparkling eyes and declared that it would be the best time of your life, because you would finally be able to do whatever you wanted. Now you realize she either has selective memory or she skipped the part where reality hit her like a brick, because no one in the middle of an existential crisis feels that euphoric.

Still, maybe she genuinely was one of those rare women who knew instantly how to fill the space. Perhaps she started painting watercolors, enrolled in French lessons, and booked a solo trip to Tuscany before the dust even settled. If so, that is her story, but it does not have to be yours. And that is perfectly fine.

Here is the first truth: you are allowed to feel like crap. Sadness is far too weak a word for the swirl of emotions that show up uninvited. It is not a graceful melancholy out of an art film, but a surreal disorientation where you wake up and feel as if you have stepped into someone else's life. You might cry for no reason in the baby food aisle, feel jealous of the mother yelling at her kids in line because at least she has something immediate to react to, or sit in your car in the driveway, unsure why you should even go inside. None of this means you are weak or dramatic. It means you are grieving, and grief is the price of loss.

The second truth: everyone lies about how quickly they got back to themselves. Social media is full of women over fifty who appear radiant and thriving, posting photos of pottery classes, mountain hikes, and tango lessons, all smiles and fulfillment, as if the empty nest instantly launched them into their best selves. What you do not see are the Tuesday afternoons when they sat in a kitchen staring into a second cup of coffee and wondering if too much caffeine counts as a problem. You do not see the evenings of eating dinner alone and feeling pathetic, or the effort of trying to make new friends now that the common ground of parenting has vanished. Stop comparing your behind-the-scenes reality to someone else's highlight reel. Their transformation may be fundamental, but it probably took far longer than their captions suggest.

The third truth: "Find your passion" is the most irritating advice ever invented. If passion were so easy to locate, there would be a drive-through window serving it with a side of fries. Passion is not a lost set of keys waiting in a drawer. For most people, it is something that develops slowly, shifts with time, and often looks more like a series of small satisfactions than one grand obsession. Your passion may not be a career-worthy calling, but instead the podcasts you enjoy while walking, the experiments with new recipes, or the so-called boring books you can finally read without interruption.

The fourth truth: you do not have to become the person you want to be overnight. Transition periods exist precisely because change is gradual. A butterfly does not emerge from a cocoon and soar with precision; it must first learn how to trust its fragile wings. In the same way, you can spend time practicing with your freedom before you decide where it should carry you.

And the fifth truth, the one that matters most: feeling lost does not mean that you are lost. It means you are in motion, and motion is evidence of life. If you felt nothing at all, if you were indifferent and numb, then you could call yourself lost. But you do feel, even if it is confusion, grief, or the strange excitement of uncertainty. Feeling means you are engaged in the process of change, and confusion is often the doorway to something new. Think back—when your children were newborns, did you know how to be a mother? On the first day of a new job, did you know exactly what to do? Of course not. You learned as you went along, and that is what you are doing again.

So the next time someone insists that you should be thrilled about this phase, you can smile politely and think to yourself: interesting perspective, but I will feel what I feel, and that is okay. You may be excited tomorrow, or next month, or next year, or your version of excitement will look nothing like theirs. That does not matter. What matters is that your journey belongs to you, and your way of walking through it is valid, whether it is filled with experiments, with grief, or with contradictions.

Today you might feel lost, and tomorrow you might too, but that does not mean you are failing. It only means that you are human and that you are in the middle of a profound shift. Permit yourself to feel exactly what you think, not what you should feel, and let that be enough for now.

Sometimes accepting that it is okay to feel lost is the first real step toward becoming found.

Exercise

Write a brutally honest social media post about how you are doing right now. Please do not share it; keep it for yourself. Then draft the version you would post for the world to see. Compare them. Notice the gap between the two. That difference is the reason why everyone else has it all figured out.

Chapter 4

Not A Breakdown, A Breakthrough — How Empty Nest Syndrome Can Become Your Launchpad

> *Amid winter, I found there was, within me, an invincible summer.*
>
> Albert Camus

The appointment you have been putting off for months finally arrives. You sit in the doctor's office, fiddling with the tissue box while she opens your chart. You rehearsed this conversation so many times, yet the words feel heavy and awkward once they leave your mouth. You confess that you are not sleeping well, that you wake up every night around four, and your brain begins running like an engine you cannot switch off, listing unfinished tasks, replaying old conversations, and worrying about things you cannot control. She nods while typing and asks how long this has been happening. You answer that it has been six months, ever since your youngest left for college, and you add quietly that just yesterday, when you heard a song your son used to play on repeat, you suddenly had to pull over because tears blurred your vision. She asks what else you are experiencing, and you admit that things you used to love no longer interest you. You even bought concert tickets you once looked forward to, but now the thought of going feels exhausting, and even reading novels have begun to feel like work.

What troubles you most is the question of whether this is depression that requires treatment or whether it is a natural response to losing the central purpose of your life. When your identity revolves around being needed every single day, what happens when that need suddenly evaporates? The doctor continues with her checklist, asking about your energy, your appetite, and your thoughts. Still, you are silently wondering whether there should not be a distinction between a chemical imbalance and the emotional earthquake that follows when your children leave home with their bags and their dreams.

Telling the difference between grief that belongs to a natural transition and depression that requires medical help is not always easy, but understanding this difference is essential if you want to give yourself the right kind of support. Many women are quick to hear suggestions about therapy or medication, and to be clear, professional help can be invaluable during a time of such upheaval. Yet it is just as important to recognize that not every tear or sleepless night is a symptom of illness. Sometimes what you are experiencing is what psychologists call *anticipatory grief*[1], the natural mourning that comes when you close a life stage that shaped your very identity.

Depression feels like being stuck in an elevator between floors, trapped in a heavy stillness that does not change for weeks or months. Transformation feels more like a long mountain journey, filled with steep climbs, rough

---

[1]Anticipatory grief refers to feelings of grief or loss that can occur before the actual loss takes place and may involve emotional stress, irritability, and other symptoms.

Healthdirect Australia. Understanding Anticipatory Grief. Accessed August 14, 2025.

paths, and unexpected fatigue, but also with glimpses of breathtaking views, and even in the most challenging stretches, there is a sense of movement forward.

There are ways to recognize whether you are in the process of transformation rather than collapse. On difficult days, your emotions still shift in color and intensity. One day it may be nostalgia for when the house was full of life, the next it may be anxiety about the future, and another day it might be a flicker of anticipation for what could come. In depression, every day remains the same shade of gray. You also retain the capacity for micro-pleasures, the small sparks of enjoyment that still reach you: the smell of fresh bread, a smile at a ridiculous meme, or the quiet satisfaction of pulling weeds from the garden. In depression, *anhedonia*[2] – the loss of ability to feel pleasure – makes even these tiny joys unreachable.

Your sleep disturbances may be frustrating, but they often reveal a connection to a change in processing. Perhaps you lie awake planning how to turn a bedroom into a guest room, or you wake up early with ideas for the weekend ahead. Depression-related sleep, by contrast, is chaotic, with no constructive thread running through it. Another sign of healthy transformation is curiosity. Even if it is fragile, you might still wonder how that new tea tastes, or whether the museum you passed still has the exhibition, or whether the online lecture you bookmarked would hold your attention. These are signals that your appetite for life still lives beneath the confusion.

Your social energy may be more selective than before. Perhaps you avoid large parties, but you still long for

---

[2]Anhedonia refers to the inability to experience pleasure or enjoyment from activities that would normally be pleasurable. Osmosis. Anhedonia. Accessed August 14, 2025.

an intimate coffee with a close friend or a meaningful conversation. In depression, the withdrawal is far more complete. You may also notice that you still plan for the future in small ways, booking a dental appointment, buying supplies for spring cleaning, or even considering a vacation. When depression takes hold, the future itself feels irrelevant or impossible to picture. Finally, even if your self-care fluctuates, it does not vanish entirely. Some days you may spend half the morning in pajamas, but on others you dress carefully and cook yourself a meal that pleases you. Depression erodes even these basic rhythms.

When you define yourself primarily through motherhood for decades, the disappearance of that role feels like the ground collapsing under you. Yet this is not destruction. It is reconstruction, and every reconstruction begins with dismantling. Think of it as renovating a house. At one point, everything is dust and exposed beams, furniture covered with cloth, walls knocked down, chaos everywhere. That does not mean the house is falling apart; it means you are in the middle of creating something better.

During this stage, you may feel like a contradiction. You are experienced, yet everything feels strangely unfamiliar. You are capable, yet clumsy like a beginner. You are wise, yet confused. This dissonance is not failure; it is the sound of growth. Of course, there are red flags that require professional help: being unable to manage basic daily activities for weeks, losing your appetite completely or eating compulsively, experiencing thoughts of self-harm, being unable to get out of bed, isolating from all social contact, or relying heavily on substances to cope.

But if you can still function, even with effort, if you still find some activities meaningful, if you catch glimpses of possibility in the future, and if your emotions move in waves rather than permanent paralysis, you are most likely in the middle of a transformation.

There are signs that you are moving forward, even if it feels slow. You notice beauty in unexpected places: the way light pours across the kitchen table, the intricate texture of tree bark, the richness of early morning silence. You develop preferences that are yours alone, independent of family dynamics: perhaps a love for documentaries instead of fiction, or a taste for spicy food you never tried when cooking for the kids, or a preference for evening walks rather than early exercise. You begin to feel emotions that exist together in complexity. You can be proud of your children's independence while missing their presence, grateful for the past while curious about what comes next, sad about the end of an era while eager to see what you might discover. You also learn self-compassion, recognizing that you cannot master a new way of living overnight, that building a new identity requires patience.

Discomfort during change is not proof of weakness. Every critical shift in your life once felt overwhelming. Your first job, your first move to a new city, even learning to drive, all required time before they felt natural. The empty nest is no different.

The distinction between breakdown and breakthrough is vital. Breakdown feels static, as though life is closing in with no way forward. Breakthrough feels like movement, sometimes painful, sometimes frightening, yet always carrying a hidden seed of possibility.

Trust your intuition about your experience. If you are worried about your mental health, seek guidance, but also trust that not every struggle signals pathology. Some of it is simply the necessary friction of becoming someone new. The discomfort you feel might not be breaking you down but shaping you into the woman you are meant to become in this next season of life.

Take a moment to reflect on the past week. Write down a single moment when you felt even the faintest spark of curiosity or interest in something new. It may have been a book title you noticed online, a place you passed and wanted to enter, an idea for an activity, or even a subject of conversation that caught your attention. Please write it down, no matter how small. That spark is evidence that your ability to engage with life is still alive and waiting for you. It is not gone; it is simply shifting toward a new expression of who you are becoming.

Chapter 5

The Loneliness Trap — How To Stop Comfort Habits From Replacing Real Life

> "*The greatest thing in the world is to know how to belong to oneself.*
> Michel de Montaigne"

It is the second week after your youngest has left for college. The house feels quiet, so quiet that the silence becomes unbearable, and you switch on the television not to watch anything in particular but to create background noise, just enough to make you feel less like the last living creature in your own home. Your husband sits in his chair, sometimes reading the newspaper, sometimes scrolling through his phone, much as he has always done, yet now the absence of the children's voices makes that silence weigh even heavier. It is no longer softened by their laughter, their questions, their complaints, or their endless movement.

Without really noticing when it happened, this has become the new normal. The television stays on from morning until night, even if nobody pays attention to it. You sit on the couch with your phone in hand, scrolling aimlessly, while he drifts somewhere else in the house. The conversations you do share are reduced to practicalities, often no more than "what's for dinner?" or "did you pay the bills?". Ordering food from an app three times in one week has begun to feel easier than cooking, because preparing a meal for two silent people at a table is sometimes more painful than cooking for one.

I call it the loneliness trap, a subtle space where you can feel profoundly alone even when sitting beside the partner you have shared twenty-five years with, a state in which the behaviors that once soothed you during the first difficult weeks slowly turn into habits that replace genuine connection, until the comfort zone solidifies into a private prison.

Many imagine that loneliness is a problem of single people, women who divorced or never married, but the truth is that loneliness can feel even sharper in marriage. Being alone in an empty house is difficult, yet at least it carries clarity. You know why you are alone, and you can consciously seek out companionship. In marriage, the contrast can be harsher: you sit next to a person who is supposed to be your closest companion, yet you cannot remember the last time you had an honest conversation about something other than bills, schedules, or plumbing repairs.

For years, the children were your main subject, the reliable thread that kept every conversation going. You talked about school, practices, teacher meetings, and sports equipment. Their lives were the bridge between you, a bridge that gave you reasons for plans, concerns, and discussions. Now that the bridge has disappeared, you are confronted with the unsettling realization that you do not know what to talk about anymore. It is not about love or respect disappearing. It is about having functioned for so long as a parenting team that you now have to rediscover how to be a couple, which is far more intimidating than it sounds. Pretending everything is fine and sitting separately with your phones seems easier than facing the strangeness of feeling like two strangers who share a house.

Loneliness in marriage is also more insidious because, from the outside, everything looks perfectly normal. You are not single, you are not visibly isolated, so the world assumes you are content. Meanwhile, the truth is that silence between two people who once shared their bed and their lives can feel more painful than silence in an empty room.

Comfort habits step in quickly to cover the discomfort. In a single household, it might be endless shows, social media, food delivery, or hours online. In a marriage, these same habits allow each partner to live in a separate bubble while still sharing the same space. He has his shows and his websites, you have your social media and your routines, and slowly you stop colliding with each other at all. The more time you spend facing a screen, the less you practice real conversation, and the less you practice conversation, the more awkward it becomes to attempt it. The more uncomfortable the attempts, the more you hide inside the easy distractions again.

It feels deceptively safe. A screen does not argue or disappoint; it keeps you entertained and fills the silence without risk. But what it does not provide is closeness, intimacy, or support. At some point, you realize that you are living more like roommates who divide the bills than as partners who share a life.

There is a fundamental difference between healthy distance and destructive distance. Healthy distance gives space for individual interests, friends, and personal time, balanced with chosen moments of connection. Destructive distance grows into a wall. You drift into separate worlds that rarely intersect, and because you are not discussing anything meaningful, you stop arguing as well. Peace exists, but it is the peace of absence, not harmony.

The warning signs are easy to recognize once you stop denying them. Evenings look the same: he in his chair with the remote, you with your laptop or phone, and the television buzzing in the background. Attempts at conversation feel uncomfortable without entertainment to fill the gaps. You plan weekends separately, vacations feel more like obligations than joy, and social media tells two completely different stories of your lives.

Escaping the loneliness trap does not happen in one leap, but in small, deliberate steps. Begin with meals: choose one time in the week when you turn off screens and share food. It may feel awkward at first, and the conversation may be limited to what is on the plate, but speaking at all is more important than the topic. Introduce one activity that belongs to both of you, whether it is a walk, a coffee outing, cooking together, or going to the cinema. Ask questions that invite more than a single-word answer. Instead of "How was work?", try "What part of your day made you feel most alive?" or "What frustrated you the most today?". Small changes in phrasing can open surprising paths to connection.

Be patient with yourselves. For years, the focus was on children and logistics, and rediscovering a deeper dialogue does not happen overnight. Intimacy rebuilds itself gradually through everyday exchanges, not through sudden declarations.

Of course, sometimes silence is not just a habit but a symptom of deeper wounds. Resentments, unresolved conflicts, or disappointments may have been pushed aside during the years of child-rearing, and now they surface. The fact that you are struggling does not mean the relationship has to end. What it often signals is the need for support in the form of therapy, mediation, or guidance that can help you both relearn how to communicate. Many couples experience such a crisis during the empty nest stage and emerge stronger than before. Others discover that they no longer share enough to continue, and though it is painful, it is also a valid truth.

There is no single outcome that defines success. Some couples fall in love again, travel together, and discover shared passions. Others part ways and build new lives. Still others remain companions in a quieter, less passionate way. Each of these directions has the potential to bring fulfillment, as long as it comes from a deliberate decision and not from passively drifting into avoidance.

What matters most is not allowing loneliness to become permanent simply because avoiding intimacy feels easier than risking it. You deserve to be seen, to be heard, and to be valued not only as a mother but as a whole woman with your own needs, thoughts, and longings. That requires leaving the safety of distraction and reaching for genuine contact. It is frightening at first, but real closeness is always worth the risk.

Exercises

1. The Background Noise Experiment

Choose one evening to turn off the television, radio, and all background noise. Notice what happens when silence fills the room. Do you feel an urge to reach for your phone? Do you want to start a conversation? Write down your emotions and how you instinctively tried to deal with the silence.

2. Real vs. Substitute Companionship

In the two columns provided, list on the left all the activities that only give you the illusion of company (scrolling social media, binge-watching shows, ordering food to avoid eating alone). On the right, list the situations that truly nourish you (talking with a friend, walking with your partner, cooking together). Compare the lists and reflect on how much of your time is spent in each.

3. One Question a Day

For one week, ask your partner one open-ended question each day–something that cannot be answered with "yes" or "no." Write down their responses, and at the end of the week, read them all together. Notice how even small doses of meaningful conversation begin to create a sense of connection.

4. The Loneliness Mirror

Sit quietly for ten minutes and write down the specific moments when you feel most lonely. Is it during meals, in the evenings, or on weekends? Then note what you usually do to fill that emptiness–scrolling, eating, or turning on the TV. Create a simple map of your habits and choose one you would like to replace with a more nourishing alternative.

5. The Micro-Connection Plan

Suggest one small but shared activity for the coming week. It can be a short walk, dinner at the table without screens, or watching a movie followed by a brief discussion. Please keep it simple so it feels realistic. Afterward, write down how you felt before, during, and after the activity.

A Note from the Author

Before you continue, I'd like to ask you for a small favor that makes a huge difference.

Did you know that reviews are the lifeblood of books like this?

They help women who are going through the same stage of life discover the support they've been searching for.

Leaving a review takes less than a minute, and it's incredibly easy:

1. Scan the QR code below to go directly to the review page.
2. Leave a quick review – just a few thoughts are enough.

Your feedback doesn't just support me, it also helps others on their journey to find the right tools and guidance.

Thank you for helping me make a difference!
Scan to leave your review on Amazon.

With love,
Natalie Huley

PART II

Rebuilding Your Nest (For One)

Chapter 6

Woman Who Lived Here Before Kids: Rediscover Who You Were Before Everyone Needed You

> *The cave you fear to enter holds the treasure you seek.*
>
> Joseph Campbell

Yesterday at the grocery store, you heard a song you loved twenty years ago. For three minutes, you danced between the canned goods aisles, hips swaying like they did in the clubs, back when all that mattered was feeling the rhythm in your bones. Then you noticed an elderly woman watching you, and in an instant, you snapped back into "respectable middle-aged woman" mode. But for those three minutes, you were yourself again, your most authentic self.

That woman who danced in the store is always there. The trouble is, you have spent years convincing yourself she should stay quiet.

Motherhood isn't just about giving life to children. It often comes with the slow, systematic silencing of parts of yourself that society deems "inappropriate" for mothers. When was the last time you said "screw it" and did something completely spontaneous? When did you last wear something sexy, not for your husband, but because you felt damn good in it? When did you last stay up late, not because a child was sick, but because you were doing something fascinating just for yourself? If it takes you longer than three seconds to think, she's been hidden away too long.

Society sold you the myth that "good mothers" stop being women. It told you they exist only as functions: transport, feeding, education, medical care, and entertainment. But there was a woman who once flirted with the bartender to see if she still could. A woman who bought lingerie no one was ever meant to see, but that transformed her and made her feel like a goddess. A woman who had opinions about politics, art, sex, and everything else unrelated to child development milestones. She was supposed to be "outgrown."

Bullshit. She didn't disappear. She's still there. Over the years, they taught her to believe she was "inappropriate." They said a mother should never see herself that way. They told her that wanting more, wanting anything for herself, was selfish. They insisted motherhood was a twenty-four-seven job with no space for any other version of her.

You can love your children beyond measure and still remember what it feels like when someone sees you not as "Tommy's mom," but as a woman who hasn't faded.

Do you remember that spark? It was when you wandered through a new city without a map, to see where the streets would take you. Maybe it was staying up until four in the morning, lost in a project that kept you so absorbed you forgot the rest of the world existed. Perhaps it was singing every word to a song you loved in your car, loud enough for people in the next lane to hear. That spark was never just a pastime. It was part of who you are.

And now that your children don't need you twenty-four hours a day, you can let that fire burn again.

But let's be honest about why this woman got hidden. It wasn't an accident. It was a calculated survival mechanism. When you became a mother, the world made it clear that your needs were now secondary. Every time you ignored a child's cry for your pleasure, you felt guilty. Every moment you spent thinking about yourself instead of the children was "proof" that you weren't a good enough mother.

So you learned to be a master of self-censorship. You stopped listening to music that reminded you of who you were before kids because it was "too loud." You stopped wearing things that emphasized your femininity because they were "impractical." You stopped having opinions about things unrelated to children because you "didn't have time to think about that stuff."

But the truth is, you had time. You just learned that time didn't belong to you.

Now comes the moment of truth: that pre-kid woman was no less responsible or no less loving than the one you became. She was just a fuller version of yourself. A version who could love deeply AND still maintain her desires. A version who could be a devoted life partner AND still flirt with life itself.

Remember what your Saturday mornings looked like before kids? Maybe you spent hours in coffee shops reading books that had no "educational value"; they just pleased you. Maybe you experimented with makeup for an hour, not because you were going somewhere special, but because you enjoyed the process of transformation. Perhaps you spent two hours on the phone with a friend, laughing until you cried over things no one else would think are funny.

Those moments weren't "wasted time." They were what made you feel alive. And when they got cut from your life in the name of "good motherhood," part of you got cut out with them.

But here's the secret nobody told you: that woman didn't disappear during those years of motherhood. She just kept herself tucked away. In the afternoons, when you took the long way home on purpose, to have ten extra minutes of quiet. In the grocery store, you slipped your favorite chocolate into the cart and didn't tell anyone.

In the mornings, when you sat in the car for a moment after parking, you finished a song before going inside. In the rare weekends when you said yes to something just because it sounded fun, not because it was "productive." She was always there, waiting.

And now, she's ready.

But reconstructing this woman isn't about resurrecting the twenty-something and pretending the last twenty years didn't happen. You're wiser now. Stronger. More aware of consequences. You have skills that the girl didn't have: you can read people, manage crises, and love unconditionally.

The goal isn't becoming who you were. The goal is to integrate who you were with who you've become, and create who you're meant to be next.

Take Sarah, a friend of mine who rediscovered herself at fifty-two. Before kids, she was the woman who would drive three hours to see a band she'd never heard of, just because the name intrigued her. After kids, she became the woman who researched every family activity to death and never did anything without checking seventeen reviews first. When her last child left for college, she realized she hadn't made a spontaneous decision in twenty years. So she bought a concert ticket that afternoon, without researching the band or reading reviews, just because she liked the poster. The music was terrible, but she felt more alive during those two hours than she had in months. Not because the experience was perfect, but because she chose it entirely for herself.

That's what reclamation is – not perfection, but permission.

So what does that look like in real life? It starts with small moments of recognition. Maybe it's picking up a lipstick in a shade you adore, not the one deemed "appropriate for your age." Perhaps it's putting on music that makes you want to move your body, not background noise for productivity. It could be wearing perfume on a regular Tuesday, not just for special occasions.

Maybe it means saying yes to invitations that sound interesting, even if they don't make "practical sense." Perhaps it means spending money on things that bring you joy, even if they're not "necessary." Maybe it means flirting: not necessarily with a specific person, but with possibilities, with life itself.

But the most significant shift is emotional. It means permitting yourself to want things again. Not just stuff for other people, but things for yourself. It means remembering that your desires matter, that your pleasure matters, that your dreams matter, not less than anyone else's, but just as much.

Yes, this process will trigger guilt. You'll wonder: "Isn't this selfish? Will my children think they weren't enough for me? Will my husband think I'm no longer a supportive wife? Will people judge me for wanting more than just family?"

Wanting more than the family role doesn't mean family wasn't enough. It means you're a complete human being with complex needs. Your children will benefit from seeing you as a whole person, not just as a function in their lives. You're showing them that women can be devoted mothers AND still have rich inner lives.

Your children learned more from watching you navigate life than from any specific thing you did for them. Now they can understand what it looks like when a woman reclaims herself, not because she wasn't happy as a mom, but because she was always more than just a mom.

People will have opinions about your choices. Some will say you're "going through a phase." Others will suggest you're "trying too hard" or that you should "act your age." But here's the truth: their discomfort with your growth is their problem, not yours. Your renaissance reminds them of things they buried about themselves.

The biggest realization might be this: the woman you were before kids wasn't someone else – she was simply the uncensored you. The you who didn't second-guess every impulse. The you who trusted her instincts about what made her happy. The you who believed she deserved good things, not because she had earned them by taking care of everyone else, but simply because she was here.

This version of you wasn't naive or immature. She connected to her desires in a way you might have forgotten. She knew the difference between wanting something and needing it. She could pursue pleasure without guilt. She could be generous with others without completely depleting herself.

These aren't character flaws to overcome. These are superpowers to reclaim.

Exercise

Think about the last time you felt genuinely attractive — not "pretty for your age" or "good for someone who's had kids," but deeply, fully attractive.

- What were you doing, and why did it matter to you?
- How were you moving – your posture, your gestures, your pace?
- What was your energy like – were you laughing more, speaking more freely?
- Who was with you, or were you alone? What made it easy to be your true self?
- What had you done for yourself that day that might have contributed to that feeling?

Now ask yourself: **what would it take to feel that way again, not just once, but often?**

Write down three small things you can do this week to reconnect with that version of yourself who knew she was attractive and wasn't afraid to show it.

Chapter 7

Your 18-Year Sabbatical Is Over — How To Reinvent Yourself After Raising Kids

> *The most common way people give up their power is by thinking they don't have any.*
>
> Alice Walker

"What are we doing with your hair today?" It's such a simple question from the stylist, but it stops you cold. For eighteen years, your automatic response has been "something practical that styles quickly." But today, something shifts. You stare in the mirror at a woman who, for years, chose hairstyles based on whether they'd look "appropriate" at parent-teacher conferences, whether they'd get in the way while helping with homework, and whether they'd be easy to maintain between trips to the dentist with the kids.

The silence stretches. Your stylist patiently waits, scissors poised, as you realize you have absolutely no idea what you want your hair to look like when you're no longer meeting everyone else's needs.

"Maybe something... different?" you say uncertainly.

The hairdresser smiles. "Different how? Shorter? Longer? Maybe some color?"

And there it is. The moment you realize how many decisions you've made based on being someone's mother first, and yourself... well, maybe never. Your hair was Mom's hair. Your clothes were mom clothes: washable, comfortable, and stain-free. Even your car was a mom car, chosen for safety ratings and cargo space, not because you loved driving it.

Now you're faced with a choice that's entirely your own, and it feels both thrilling and terrifying. What if you hate it? What if people think you're having a midlife crisis? But... what if you love it?

And suddenly it hits you with shocking clarity: you don't remember what kind of hair you like. For nearly two decades, every decision about your appearance was made through the lens of what was "practical for a mom." And now, suddenly, you can look exactly how you want. The problem is, you don't remember what you want.

Neuroscience has a name for what's happening to you: learned helplessness in the context of your autonomy.[3] For years, your brain was trained to respond to external cues - children's needs, family schedules, social expectations about being a "good mother." Your neural pathways became so deeply carved into patterns of serving others that when those external triggers fade, you feel lost when making decisions for yourself.

Research by Dr. Martin Seligman shows that when people are in situations where they have no control over

---

[2]Martin E. P. Seligman, "Learned Helplessness," Annual Review of Medicine 23 (1972): 407–412.

their environment for extended periods, their brains reprogram themselves in ways that make them believe they have no power even when they've regained it.[4] This is precisely what happened to you through years of motherhood.

For eighteen years, you lived in a constant state of what psychologists call "hypervigilance for others." Your nervous system was on permanent alert for everyone else's needs. Brain imaging studies of mothers show that motherhood changes brain structure – areas responsible for anxiety and empathy can grow by up to twenty percent, while areas related to self-focus often shrink from lack of use.[5]

You're not to blame for this. It's biological adaptation that made evolutionary sense – mothers who were hypersensitive to their offspring's needs were more likely to pass on their genes. But now that you no longer need to be on high alert for someone else, your brain doesn't know how to return to "me first" mode.

And here's the fascinating part: research shows this neuroplasticity works both ways.[6] Just as your brain adapted to constant caregiving, it can also readapt to self-direction. But it needs deliberate practice, like a muscle after an injury requires physical therapy.

What you're experiencing has its place in the developmental cycle. Identity research shows a consistent pattern: the

---

4. Ibid.

5 Pilyoung Kim, James F. Leckman, Linda C. Mayes, Ruth Feldman, Xian Wang, and James E. Swain, "The Plasticity of Human Maternal Brain: Longitudinal Changes in Brain Anatomy during the Early Postpartum Period," Behavioral Neuroscience 124, no. 5 (2010): 695–700.

6 Norman Doidge, The Brain That Changes Itself: Stories of Personal Triumph from the Frontiers of Brain Science (New York: Viking, 2007).

first few months after children leave are characterized by what psychologists call "decision paralysis" – an inability to make even simple choices about how to live.[7]

Your brain doesn't have established neural highways for making decisions based purely on your preferences. Those pathways existed before children, but they've been "overgrown" through years of disuse, like a forest path that's no longer used.

Research on neurological recovery shows that rebuilding these pathways requires a specific type of practice. You need to deliberately exercise your "choice muscle" in low-stakes situations to restore confidence in your decision-making.

Start with what scientists call "autonomy micro-practices." [8] Studies show that small, consistent acts of self-direction are more effective at brain reprogramming than big, overwhelming decisions.

Here's what these micro-practices look like in daily life perfect:)

Morning choices:	Transportation decisions:
Instead of automatically making the same breakfast you've made for years, pause and ask what you're hungry for.	Take a different route somewhere – not because it's more efficient, but because you want to see what's down that street you've driven past a thousand times.

[7] Barbara A. Mitchell and Linda D. Lovegreen, "The Empty Nest Syndrome in Midlife Families: A Multigenerational Perspective," Canadian Journal on Aging 28, no. 4 (2009): 475–490.

[8] B. J. Fogg, Tiny Habits: The Small Changes That Change Everything (Boston: Houghton Mifflin Harcourt, 2019).

Clothing experiments:

Wear something that makes you feel good rather than what's most practical.

Entertainment choices:

Watch a movie or TV show that interests you, even if nobody else in your household would enjoy it.

Social experiments:

Sit in a different spot at your regular coffee shop.

Food adventures:

Buy something at the grocery store that you've always been curious about but never tried.

Time experiments:

Spend an hour doing something completely "unproductive."

Neuroscientists have discovered that authentic pleasure-seeking behavior – when it's not compulsive – strengthens neural pathways related to self-awareness and decision-making.[9] When you do things purely for your enjoyment, your brain releases dopamine in areas connected to motivation and goal-setting.

"Treating yourself" isn't selfish; it's a neurological necessity for rebuilding your ability to live with autonomy.

Studies of midlife transition reveal a fascinating phenomenon: women who successfully navigate the empty nest period often develop what psychologists

---

[9] Doidge, The Brain That Changes Itself.

[10] Mitchell and Lovegreen, "The Empty Nest Syndrome in Midlife Families."

call "enhanced executive function." [10] All those years managing complex family logistics strengthened parts of the brain related to planning, problem-solving, and multitasking.

But you've been using these superpowers only in the service of others. Research shows that when these cognitive abilities are redirected toward personal goals, women often achieve remarkable things in the second half of life – more than they ever imagined possible.[11]

Dr. Erik Erikson, a pioneer in developmental psychology, identified this exact stage: "generativity versus stagnation." [12] The challenge isn't just adapting to an empty nest – it's discovering how to channel your generative energy toward purposes that fulfill you personally, not just serve others.

Women who thrive at this stage often report feeling more authentic and capable than ever before. But first, they must go through a period of neurological readjustment.

Practical advice based on brain science: each day, ask yourself not "what should I do?" but "what would feel satisfying right now?" Then do it, even if it seems trivial.

Your brain needs practice recognizing and following your impulses rather than external demands.

---

[11] bid.

[12] Erik H. Erikson, Childhood and Society (New York: W. W. Norton & Company, 1950).

According to research from University College London, creating new neural pathways and making them automatic requires an average of sixty-six days of consistent practice.[13]

Studies also show that social connections based on shared interests - rather than shared obligations - are crucial for this transition.[14] Your brain needs to experience relationships where you're valued for who you are, not what you do for others.

Research in positive psychology shows that this transitional period - though difficult - often leads to what scientists call "posttraumatic growth." [15]

Many women report that the empty nest period becomes a launching pad for the most satisfying chapter of their lives - but only when they actively engage in the process of neurological reprogramming rather than waiting for it to happen naturally.

---

[14] Mitchell and Lovegreen, "The Empty Nest Syndrome in Midlife Families."

[15] Richard G. Tedeschi and Lawrence G. Calhoun, "The Posttraumatic Growth Inventory: Measuring the Positive Legacy of Trauma," Journal of Traumatic Stress 9, no. 3 (1996): 455–471.

[13] Phillippa Lally, Cornelia H. M. Van Jaarsveld, Henry W. W. Potts, and Jane Wardle, "How Are Habits Formed: Modelling Habit Formation in the Real World," European Journal of Social Psychology 40, no. 6 (2010): 998–1009.

Exercise

Letter from the Future

Imagine that your future self – the one who has already rediscovered her identity after the kids left – is writing you a letter. How does she describe her life now? Which choices turned out to be the turning points? What advice does she give you to begin today? Write this letter in your handwriting, and then read it aloud so you can hear your "future self" more clearly.

Chapter 8

The Clock Stops Here — Taking Back Your Time (And Actually Enjoying It)

> *Time is what we want most,*
> *but what we use worst.*
> William Penn

The ATM receipt shows $3,247. Not a fortune, but decent. You fold it carefully, already planning: maybe new furniture for the living room, perhaps some minor renovations, save it for vacation. Every dollar matters, and every decision is thoughtful.

You walk back to your car, mentally calculating whether you can afford both the new couch and the weekend getaway, when a thought hits you like cold water: **have you ever thought about your time like an account balance?**

At fifty, if you're lucky enough to live to eighty-five, you have roughly 306,600 hours left. Sounds like a lot, right? But subtract sleep: about 102,200 hours. If you're still working, you'll need to work another 62,400 hours over the next fifteen years–routine maintenance of life: shopping, cleaning, appointments, errands... easily

50,000 more hours. Suddenly, you're looking at 92,000 hours of truly discretionary time left in your entire life—less than what you've already spent sleeping in the past decade.

You wouldn't spend $3,247 without thinking twice, yet how many of those precious hours have you frittered away on things that don't matter? Scrolling mindlessly, watching shows you don't even enjoy, saying yes to obligations that drain you, staying in conversations that go nowhere?

The brutal math of mortality hits different when your kids are gone before and you realize that, for the first time in decades, how you spend your remaining hours is entirely up to you.

Those 92,000 hours aren't getting a refill. There's no overtime opportunity to earn more time. It's your final account balance, and it's not negotiable.

This year, you have 8,760 hours to spend. That's your time account. And unlike money, you can't earn more time—once you waste an hour, you permanently withdraw it and can never put it back.

For years, you spent this time like someone with an unlimited credit card: handing out hours to anyone who asked, without checking your balance or considering returns. But now, for the first time, you can be a strategic investor of your own 8,760 hours.

The question is: what returns do you want to achieve?

Meet Helen, 52 years old. When her last child left home three years ago, Helen was the classic empty nester: lost, directionless, spending whole days on mindless activities.

But then she calculated: "I have about 5,000 waking hours per year. If I waste 3 hours daily, I'll waste 1,095 hours in a year."

1,095 hours. That's equivalent to working full-time for 6 months.

Helen decided to invest these hours differently. She'd always been fascinated by genealogy, but "never had time." She spent 500 hours in the first year researching her family history. She discovered ancestors she never knew, uncovered family mysteries, and connected with distant relatives around the world.

Third year? Helen runs a thriving genealogy consultation business, helps other families discover their roots, and has just finished writing a book about her family saga. Her time investment gave her a new career, a new passion, and a new sense of purpose.

Five hundred hours changed her life. That's 1.4 hours daily for a year.

Or meet Patricia, 49. After the kids left, Patricia spent the first months in total depression. But then she realized something: for 20 years, she'd only sung lullabies and Disney songs. Her voice, which was once her pride, had been unused for decades.

Patricia invested 2 hours daily (730 hours per year) in vocal training, joining the local choir, and taking music lessons. Sounds like a lot? That's less than 15% of her available time.

Second year? Patricia performs regularly with community theater. Third year? She starts giving voice lessons to other women her age. Fourth year? Patricia releases her first album of classic song covers, with profits supporting local children's music programs.

Seven hundred thirty hours annually transformed her from a silent mother to a performing artist.

Meet Margaret, 55. Margaret always loved fitness, but years of driving kids to sports led her to stop exercising herself. After the empty nest, she felt weak, tired, and frustrated with her body.

Margaret decided to invest 1 hour daily (365 hours annually) in physical fitness. Nothing revolutionary, right? But Margaret didn't go to a regular gym. Instead, she trained for things she always wanted to try: rock climbing, hiking, and eventually mountaineering.

Third year? Margaret summited Mount Whitney. Fourth year? She leads hiking groups for women over 50. Fifth year? Margaret opens an outdoor adventure company specifically for middle-aged women who want to discover their strength.

Three hundred sixty-five hours annually gave her a stronger body, a new community, and business ventures. What do these women have in common? None made radical overnight changes. None quit everything and started completely over. Instead, each took a specific portion of their daily hours and invested them strategically in something meaningful.

Helen: 1.4 hours daily

Patricia: 2 hours daily

Margaret: 1 hour daily

And each completely transformed her life.

Now consider a typical day: how many hours do you spend watching TV shows that fail to inspire you?

Scrolling through social media posts that irritate you? Engaging in conversations that drain your energy? Doing things out of habit rather than intention?

If you spend even 2 hours daily on meaningless activities, that's 730 hours annually. Enough to learn a new language fluently. Enough to get certified in a new skill. Enough to write a novel. Enough to train for a marathon.

But what if you don't know what you want to invest your time in? Start with an exploration phase. Permit yourself to try different investments without long-term commitment.

Janet, 51, spent the first 6 months testing different "time investments." 50 hours on pottery classes (loved it). 40 hours on a photography course (not her thing). I volunteered for 30 hours at an animal shelter (absolutely loved it). 60 hours learning Italian (fascinating). 45 hours on a garden design workshop (discovered hidden passion).

By year's end, Janet knew precisely where she wanted to invest her time going forward: advanced pottery, expanded volunteering, and garden design certification. Her exploration investment paid off with clear direction for the future.

Linda, 54, took a different approach. Instead of trying new things, she deep-dived into something she always loved but never had proper time for: cooking. But instead of just cooking for family, Linda invested 3 hours daily studying culinary arts seriously.

Year one: mastered French techniques. Year two: specialized in pastry arts. Year three: opened a small catering business from home. Year four: teaches cooking classes and writes a food blog. Year five: published a cookbook and had TV appearances.

One thousand ninety-five hours annually transformed a hobby into an expertise into a business.

Here's the key insight: your time investment doesn't have to be career-focused. Some women invest in relationships, some in personal growth, some in creative expression, some in physical challenges, some in spiritual development.

Maria, 53, invested her time in becoming a better friend. Instead of surface-level coffee dates, she scheduled regular 3-hour deep conversation sessions with people she truly cared about. Result? Stronger, more meaningful relationships and a reputation as someone people trust with their deepest concerns.

Susan, 48, invested in becoming an expert on her neighborhood. She spent hours walking different streets, talking to longtime residents, researching local history, and visiting all local businesses. Result? She became an unofficial neighborhood ambassador, started a successful blog about local culture, and feels deeply connected to her community.

The point isn't the specific activity. The fact is, strategic thinking about how you spend your time and what returns you want.

Here's your homework: Over the next week, track exactly where your hours go. Not judgmentally, just factually.

Then ask yourself: "If I were an investor reviewing this portfolio, would I be satisfied with the returns?"

If the answer is no, you know it's time for reallocation.

Your 8,760 hours this year are a finite resource. But they're also an incredible opportunity. In economics, return on investment is one of the most critical metrics. In life, return on time investment might be even more important.

You can rebuild a career. You can build new relationships. You can develop new skills. You can discover new passions. You can create a legacy. You can transform not just your own life, but other people's lives.

All it takes is a strategic investment of a particular portion of your daily hours.

Helen, Patricia, Margaret, Janet, Linda, Maria, and Susan: none were extraordinary women. They just made extraordinary decisions about how to spend their time.

The question isn't "do you have enough time." The question is: "Are you ready to invest it wisely?"

Your 8,760-hour portfolio awaits your decision.

TIME INVESTMENT: Exercises

Exercise 1: Your Time Portfolio

Track your hours for one week. Break them into three categories:

- **Investment Hours** – time that builds something meaningful (growth, health, passions, relationships).
- **Maintenance Hours** – daily life tasks (shopping, cleaning, bills).
- **Lost Hours** – time spent on things that give you nothing in return.
- Look at your "time portfolio" and ask: Does it match what matters to me?

Exercise 2: The 100-Hour Challenge

Pick something you've always wanted to do but "never had time for." Learning a language? Painting? Yoga?

Commit to giving it **100 hours over the next 6 months.**

That's just 50 minutes a day. Watch how focused time changes everything.

Exercise 3: The What-If Calculator

Ask yourself: "*What if I had spent these hours differently?*"

Example: 2 hours of TV a night = 730 hours a year. That's enough to:

- learn a new language
- write a book

- train for a marathon
- Write down your own "what ifs." One of them might spark something big

Exercise 4: The Legacy Test
Ask yourself: "*What do I want to be remembered for in 10 years?*"

Do you want to be the woman who always dares to try new things? The one who found her passion? The one who built deep connections?

Then work backwards: how many hours a week would it take to build that legacy? Start investing them now.

(Tip: if 10 years feels too far, shrink it to 3.)

Exercise 5: The 30-Minute Magic
Pick something that excites you, even a little. Give it just **30 minutes a day**. Painting, dancing, writing–whatever. That's 182 hours in a year: small steps, significant change.

Document your progress–photos, notes, short videos. Seeing how far you've come will keep you moving.

These aren't "to-do list" chores. They're little reinvestments of your time account–so you can get real returns in joy, growth, and meaning.

Chapter 9

Your Style, Your Rules — Dressing With Midlife Confidence, Not Mom Guilt

> *Style is a way to say who you are without having to speak.*
>
> Rachel Zoe

The fluorescent lights in the dressing room are merciless, yet this deep red dress changes everything. Your eyes sparkle, your skin glows, and for the briefest moment, you hardly recognize the woman reflected in the mirror. The dress is beautiful, elegant, and demanding of attention, and that is precisely why your hand hesitates on the hanger, as if ready to return it to the rack before it exposes too much of you.

For more than two decades, you have chosen clothes by one guiding principle: they must be neutral, practical, and unremarkable enough to guarantee invisibility. Beige sweaters that could hide stains, black trousers that matched everything and revealed nothing, shoes that were comfortable enough to carry you from school pick-up to late-night rehearsals, all in colors so muted they almost apologized for existing. Your wardrobe became a language of restraint, whispering: please, do not notice me, I am only here to do my job.

The choice was not accidental. It was a survival strategy during the years when children were in middle and high school, and every detail of a mother's behavior seemed to matter. Most women adopted a kind of stylistic camouflage without ever speaking about it aloud. The goal was to blend into the background of bleachers, classrooms, and committee meetings. It was safer not to stand out, not to risk a child's embarrassment in front of friends who judged mercilessly, not to be labeled as a mother who tried too hard or wanted to compete with her daughter. Dressing became an exercise in disappearing gracefully, a performance of responsibility and acceptability.

And for a long time, it worked. You managed to live within the boundaries of expectation. You became reliable, appropriate, the woman no one questioned.

But this red dress disrupts the rules. It refuses to blend in, refuses to apologize, refuses to hide. It calls attention to itself and, by extension, to you. It suggests that the woman who wears it has a life beyond school gyms and parent conferences. It insists she has a story worth telling. When was the last time you bought something simply because you loved it, rather than because it was safe?

When was the last time you stood before a mirror and thought, I look beautiful, instead of, at least I won't embarrass anyone? When did you stop dressing for yourself and start dressing for social acceptance, for your children's comfort, for the convenience of hurried mornings when there was no time to think?

Over the years, without ever naming it, you constructed an invisibility uniform. Rows of neutral blazers, sweaters in muted shades, practical shoes. Clothing that worked everywhere but expressed nothing. A wardrobe that made you efficient, responsible, and unnoticeable, but no longer allowed you to feel visible to yourself.

Now, with children grown or nearly grown, the rules no longer apply. No one sits in the car commenting on your choices. No one cares at the bleachers whether you appear appropriately modest or slightly overdressed. The only person you must consider now is yourself, and that realization can be both liberating and terrifying.

For many women, the problem is that after years of neutrality, they do not remember what their style once was. You have lost the connection. Two decades of choosing comfort and safety over self-expression created closets full of garments that serve functions but reveal nothing of the woman who owns them. They stand before those closets searching for themselves and finding only a collection of serviceable pieces that belong to no one in particular.

That is why moments like this, holding a red dress under fluorescent lights, feel so startling. The gap between the woman you are and the wardrobe you have constructed is suddenly visible. You realize you have clothes for every parental duty but nothing that celebrates you, nothing that allows you to feel elegant, feminine, or fully alive.

Although this discovery may feel unsettling, it is also an invitation. You now have the chance to rediscover who you are stylistically, not as a girl learning herself for the first time but as a woman in midlife, with wisdom, confidence, and resources she never possessed before. Yes, it is sobering to recognize that you placed your love of beauty, color, and fabric into hibernation for so long, yet it is equally thrilling to know you can awaken it again.

The first step is honesty. As you look through your clothes, ask whether each item was chosen out of love or necessity, whether it expresses who you are, or whether it simply solved a practical problem. Most of what you own belongs to the realm of background clothing, garments designed to offend no one and reveal nothing.

It is not your fault. For years, such choices made sense. They were the armor required to navigate the unspoken rules of parenthood and the constant scrutiny of others. But those rules no longer govern you. You are free to write new ones.

Rediscovering your style does not mean trying to look younger or desperately imitating trends meant for women half your age. It means learning how to honor the woman you are now, with this body, this life, this experience. It means choosing colors that illuminate your skin, shapes that flatter your figure today, fabrics that make you feel sensual and alive. It means asking not whether something is socially acceptable but whether it makes you feel radiant.

And when you begin to make choices in that spirit, everything changes. Dressing ceases to be a chore or a way of disappearing. It becomes a declaration that you exist, that you matter, that you are willing to be visible.

Because in the end, this red dress is not merely fabric. It is a question waiting for your answer. Are you ready to stop hiding? Are you prepared to be seen again, not as the efficient background figure in everyone else's story, but as the vivid main character in your own?

You glance once more at your reflection, at the woman in red who feels both unfamiliar and entirely like you. The hanger is still in your hand, but now you know the truth: the decision is not about buying a dress. It is about deciding whether you are finally ready to step out of the background and claim the stage of your own life.

STYLE RENAISSANCE: Exercises

Exercise 1: "Style Memory Archaeology "

Dig out photos of yourself from before you had kids: high school, college, early twenties. Look at what you loved wearing back then. What colors dominated your wardrobe? What styles made you feel most confident? What accessories did you always reach for? Which of these elements reflected your authentic personality versus what was trendy at the time? Identify three style elements from your pre-motherhood years that you could reintroduce now, updated for your current age and lifestyle. The goal isn't to recreate old looks, but to reconnect with the style instincts you had before practicality took over.

Exercise 2: "Compliment Collection"

For one whole month, pay attention to every compliment you receive about your appearance: from strangers, friends, family, coworkers. Write them down immediately, including what you were wearing and how you felt that day. Also, note when you feel most confident and attractive, even if no one comments. At the end of the month, analyze the patterns: What colors, styles, or looks consistently get positive reactions? What makes people say "you look great" versus "you look nice"? Use these insights to understand what works for you now, not what you think should work.

Exercise 3: "Style Confidence Challenge"

Each week for a month, wear one thing that feels slightly "too much" for your everyday routine: a brighter color than usual, a more fitted silhouette, a bolder accessory, or a dressier outfit for a casual occasion. Notice how wearing something that pushes your comfort zone affects your mood, posture, and energy throughout the day. Please pay attention to how others respond to you and whether their reactions match your fears about standing out. Document how your definition of "too much" evolves as you get more comfortable with being noticed.

Exercise 4: "Shopping With New Eyes"

Go on a shopping trip with only one rule: you must buy something that makes you genuinely smile when you see it, regardless of practicality or whether it "goes with everything."

It could be a bright scarf, interesting earrings, a beautiful top, or unique shoes. The item doesn't have to be expensive, but it has to spark joy and feel like "you." Notice how it feels to choose based on attraction rather than function. Then, wear your purchase and observe how owning something you love (not just need) affects your relationship with your appearance.

Exercise 5: "Style Evolution Journal "

Take a photo of yourself each week as you rediscover your style. Include a brief note about how you felt that day, what you tried that was new or different, and your confidence level from 1-10. After three months, review all the photos and notes. What patterns do you see? Which experiments worked best? How has your confidence evolved? What style direction seems most authentically "you"? Use this visual and emotional record to guide your ongoing style development and celebrate how far you've come in reclaiming your aesthetic.

Chapter 10

Your Second Virginity — Dating, Intimacy, And Desire After 50

> *The body benefits from movement, and the mind benefits from stillness. But the soul benefits from desire.*
>
> Rumi

You're standing in front of your bedroom mirror, you're not checking for stains on your blouse before a parent-teacher conference, not glancing to see if your hair looks good enough for your teenager's game. You're simply looking at a woman. At your body. At your hips, no longer defined by carrying bags of sports equipment and emergency changes of clothes, and at your lips, no longer occupied with saying "no" and enforcing curfews.

And suddenly something strikes you, both shocking and liberating: for the first time in twenty years, you are just a woman again. Not a mom-taxi, not a wife managing teenage crises, but simply a woman who is unsure what that even means anymore.

For years, your body had one purpose: serving others. It carried heavy bags, sat for hours on bleachers during games, and endured endless car rides to tournaments.

Your hands checked for fevers after late-night parties, your arms offered hugs after heartbreaks, and your knees stayed hidden under safe skirts because you wondered what people would think of a mother wearing something short. Your body was a tool of motherhood, reliable, available, always dressed appropriately, but it was not a body you desired. Perhaps your husband did, briefly, between arguments about curfews and messy rooms, but you didn't. When was the last time you looked at your body and thought of it not as a vehicle, but as a source of pleasure?

And now you face a question that feels both frightening and necessary: who are you as a sexual being when no one needs you as a driver, negotiator, or crisis manager anymore? It's a question many women never voice aloud, but it lingers silently in the minds of those who have reached the empty nest. For years, you absorbed society's message that mothers of teenagers are not sexy, that motherhood and sexuality cannot coexist, that once you enter that role, you automatically become an asexual guardian whose main job is to make sure children don't have sex too early. You knew it was nonsense, but for years you lived as if it were true. And now, with the noise of parenting quieted, you feel like a woman who has forgotten her language.

Do you remember yourself before motherhood? The woman who wore lace lingerie not because someone would see it, but because she loved how it felt against her skin. The woman bought perfume because it made her feel sensual. The woman who could spend an hour in the bathtub without worrying someone would burst in needing help with tomorrow's outfit. Practical motherhood buried that woman under layers: sports bras for bleacher seating, clothes chosen for encounters with teachers, hairstyles crafted for meetings with school psychologists, and makeup applied to look respectable when speaking to police about weekend mishaps.

For years, you chose your appearance based on appropriateness rather than beauty. And desire had no room to breathe. How can you think about sex when you're waiting at one in the morning for your teenager to come home? You can't feel sensual when you spend the day uncovering lies or negotiating rules. You can't want intimacy when you fall asleep clutching your phone, waiting for a call that might announce disaster. Your vigilance and responsibility drowned your libido in endless noise, but they never destroyed it.

Now there is silence. And in that silence, you begin to hear a voice you thought had gone forever. Yesterday, standing before your closet, you lingered longer than usual. Not because you didn't know what to wear, but because you asked a new question: *What makes me feel beautiful*? Not *What will be appropriate if I run into other parents*, not *What will be practical for a day of managing crises*, but simply *What makes me feel like a woman*?

Your hand reached for a silk blouse you bought years ago and never wore because it felt too luxurious, too indulgent for a mother juggling schedules and carpools. When you slipped it on, the smooth fabric against your skin awakened something you hadn't felt in years. You felt sensual. And that scared you. What do you mean when you think alluring once your days no longer revolve around managing teenage chaos?

It feels like a second virginity, the rediscovery of yourself as a sexual being. But unlike the first time, now you have wisdom. You know what you want. You know what you like. You know your worth has nothing to do with other people's opinions. And most importantly, you know you have the right not only to be desired but also to desire, to desire desire itself.

You can think of your body not as a machine that transports, manages, and endures, but as a source of sensation. You can touch your skin not to check for stress rashes, but to appreciate its softness. You can look in the mirror not to assess whether you appear "appropriate," but to admire your curves.

You can redefine what it means to be sexy. Perhaps sexy is not the twenty-year-old girl with no idea what she wants, but the woman who endured the storms of teenage motherhood and survived. Possibly sexy is the confidence of someone who knows she can face anything because she has already faced it. Perhaps sexy is the calm of a woman who no longer has to worry whether her children will return home safely, because they are now responsible for themselves.

Maybe sexy is you, exactly as you are now.

This realization is not easy. For decades, you have been bombarded with the idea that women over fifty are invisible, that their desirability has expired, that they should retreat into roles of grandmotherly wisdom and leave sexuality behind—more nonsense. Your sexuality doesn't have an expiration date. It evolves. It matures. It becomes more authentic. For so long, your children absorbed most of your strength, and your husband took what remained, but now you hold the freedom to uncover what genuinely delights you.

And this is where the adventure begins. You may discover that your body responds differently than it did in your twenties, slower to ignite but deeper, richer once it does. You may find that intimacy is no longer about quick release between crises, but about closeness, exploration, and play. You may realize that your sexuality doesn't even need another person to be complete. That you finally have the time and space to discover your own body, to learn what delights you without pressure to satisfy anyone else.

The most liberating part of your second virginity may be that you don't need to be sexy for anyone else. You can be sexy for yourself. You can buy lingerie no one will see, simply because it makes you feel powerful. You can take long baths with oils and candles, not in preparation for anyone, but as a gift to yourself. You can dance in your bedroom to music that stirs your soul. You can wear perfume that excites you, touch your body with tenderness, and honor all that it has carried you through.

Paradoxically, when you begin to be sexy for yourself, others notice. Not because you are trying, but because confidence radiates. The confidence of a woman who has survived the hardest years of motherhood is magnetic. People begin to look at you differently, speak to you differently, and sense your energy. You are no longer just "someone's mom." You are a woman.

Because when a woman knows she is beautiful and desirable, the world reflects it.

And yet the most essential truth in all of this is that you are not doing it for them. You are not proving anything, not chasing lost time, not performing for an audience.

You are reclaiming what was always yours: your right to be a sexual, sensual, fully alive woman.

Your sexuality is not a relic of youth. It is one of the greatest gifts you can offer yourself at this stage of life, a celebration of being here, breathing, feeling, thriving.

Your second virginity is not about going back to who you were before children. It is about becoming someone new, a woman seasoned with experience, lit by wisdom, alive with passion. You survived the chaos of raising teenagers. Now it is time for the reward.

Are you ready to begin? Your body is.

SEXUALITY DISCOVERY: Exercises

Exercise 1: "A New Look"

For one week, spend ten minutes a day in front of the mirror. Look at yourself not as "the former mom of teenagers," but as a woman reclaiming her body and herself. Don't search for flaws. Search for features that are uniquely yours. Notice what you like, what you want to reclaim, and what you want to explore again. If your thoughts slip into criticism, bring them back to what sparks pride or tenderness.

Exercise 2: "Sensory Inventory"

Make a list of everything that gives you pleasure through your five senses: touch, smell, taste, sound, sight. Over the next week, give yourself at least one of these pleasures every day. Pay attention to which ones you've neglected for years – and ask yourself why.

Exercise 3: "Something Just for You"

Buy one thing that makes you feel beautiful or special, even if no one else will ever see it. It could be a silk nightgown, a quality body cream, a soft scarf, or lingerie that makes you feel like a goddess. The point is to choose it solely for your pleasure, without worrying about what's "appropriate" for your age.

Exercise 4: "Private Dance"

Find music that moves you from the inside out. Close the door, dim the lights, light a candle, and dance the way your body wants to move, not the way it "should." There's no choreography, no judgment–just movement, and how it feels in your skin.

Exercise 5: "The Woman You're Becoming"

Write a letter to yourself about the woman you're becoming, not the mother you were. Describe what you want to try, what you want to discover, and how you want to feel in your own body. Don't look back at old limitations. Look ahead at possibilities.

Chapter 11

Money, Honey — How To Make, Manage, And Multiply Your Midlife Freedom Fund

> *A woman must have money and a room of her own.*
>
> Virginia Woolf

Remember that moment? Your kid packed the last bag, you hugged goodbye, and suddenly you were alone in a house that felt too big and far too quiet. And then, maybe over coffee or maybe over wine, you opened your bank account and thought: "Okay... so now what?" For the first time in two decades, you didn't have to check if there was enough for another school supply run, summer camp fee, or one of those "emergency" car repairs that always came at the worst possible moment.

If your financial decisions for the past twenty years revolved around cleats, name-brand jeans, and endless kid-related costs, welcome to the club of millions of women who are just discovering that their money can finally serve them. No more "Mom, can I have twenty bucks for lunch?" This time, your paycheck doesn't have to vanish into other people's dreams about the latest phone.

Forget about the so-called "rainy day fund" that always disappeared anyway on school trips or dentist appointments. It's time for a freedom fund – money for your life, your dreams, your "what if I finally did that thing?" For the trips you envied in friends' vacation photos. For that photography class you kept postponing until "later." For plan B, plan C, and even plan "what if I just opened that flower shop I dreamed about before my first pregnancy?"

Here's the truth nobody tells you: financial independence is the sharpest filter you'll ever have. When you don't need to accept every offer out of desperation, when you're not worried about every bill, you can choose from strength instead of fear.

You've probably heard the "pay yourself first" rule[16], but when most of your income went to rent, food, and children, it sounded like fantasy. Paying yourself first doesn't mean buying a purse before covering rent, or splurging on things that don't matter. It means that before you pay bills or calculate what's left for the month, you set aside a percentage for yourself – for your future, your security, your freedom. Start with ten percent, no exceptions, no "better month," no excuses. If your kids could reliably pay for streaming services and takeout apps, you can reliably fund your own savings account.

And let's be honest. The job market after fifty isn't kind. Some employers will glance at your age and not your skills. They'll assume you're slow with technology (even if you run circles around their twenty-something interns on a smartphone) or that you won't be "flexible" (as if two

---

[16] Popular personal finance principles promoted by George S. Clason in The Richest Man in Babylon (1926) and later by financial advisors such as David Bach.

decades of juggling work, kids, and crises weren't the ultimate flexibility test). That doesn't mean you're stuck. It means you need to get creative and lean into your strengths – experience, reliability, emotional intelligence, and the ability to keep going when others panic.

For years, you've been the household's chief organizer, crisis manager, negotiator, and multitasking wizard. Companies pay good money for people who can take a project from chaos to completion – exactly the skill set you mastered while coordinating family life. The secret is learning to translate "kept three teenagers alive and functioning" into business language.

Freelancing and consulting can be a natural first step. Writing, graphics, project management, coaching, helping younger moms get organized – people pay for what you did for decades for free. And they pay well, because they know an experienced woman who survived teenage drama can handle any deadline. You may not immediately earn what you once did, but an extra $500 or $1,000 a month is already freedom.

Passion-based businesses are another option, though they take patience. The crocheted pillows you made for fun could sell online. The cakes you baked for birthdays might grow into a small catering business. The patience you had teaching math could become tutoring that parents gladly pay for.

A friend of mine spent fifteen years organizing birthday parties for her kids. She expected to finish when the youngest turned eighteen, but she used her skills to start planning events for local companies. They quickly realized that someone who could wrangle thirty kids could handle a hundred employees. Year one, she barely covered costs. Year two, she saw real profit. By year three, she was earning more than in her old corporate job, with the freedom to choose her projects.

Money management isn't punishment, and a budget isn't a diet you break at the first temptation. A budget is simply a map so your money doesn't disappear as quickly as your teenagers did when they turned eighteen. For years, your budget was: "money comes in, money goes to kids, house, bills, let's see what's left." Now you can do it differently.

Managing your money with the 50/30/20 rule[17] is far simpler than juggling three kids' calendars. Fifty percent for fixed costs: rent, food, and bills. Thirty percent for pleasures: dinners out, books, classes, and massages.

Twenty percent for the future: savings, investments, security. Add one simple monthly ritual: fifteen minutes with coffee to check your balance, note significant expenses, and set next month's goals. No guilt about cappuccinos, no overanalyzing receipts. Just awareness.

Investing sounds intimidating, but the basics are more straightforward than teaching a teen to do laundry. A savings account with interest is the first step. Index funds[18] are like a basket of companies you buy and hold.

You don't need to understand every stock abbreviation – you need patience and realistic expectations. The most significant return, though, is in yourself: courses, certificates, skills that bring you joy and extra income.

---

[17] Budgeting method popularized by U.S. Senator Elizabeth Warren and Amelia Warren Tyagi in All Your Worth: The Ultimate Lifetime Money Plan (2005).

[18] Index funds were pioneered by John C. Bogle, founder of Vanguard Group, and have become a widely recommended long-term investment tool.

Watch for traps. If someone promises "quick profit without risk," run. If it sounds too good to be true, it is. Don't let your savings vanish faster than snacks in your kitchen after school.

For years, you automatically said "we can't afford it" when it came to your desires – the dance class, the spa weekend, the clothes you wanted. Somehow, there was always money for camps, consoles, or the latest shoes. That mindset has to change. Your needs matter as much as anyone's.

Learning to say "no" is part of this new financial power. "No, I won't fund your endless career changes." "No, I won't lend money to your son's half-baked business idea." "No, I don't have to explain why I bought something for myself." Saying no isn't selfish. It's survival. Your children won't finance your life at seventy – so you need to.

Now imagine yourself in ten years. How do you want to live? Where do you want to live? What do you want your days to look like? Create three versions of your future: minimal, comfortable, and luxury. Minimal: basic needs, small pleasures, security. Comfortable: travel once or twice a year, classes, and helping your kids without sacrificing yourself. Luxury: complete freedom to do what you want, when you want, without looking at the price.

Run the numbers. You may be surprised how close "comfortable" or even "luxury" actually is, especially if you start today. Plan for surprises too – health issues, aging parents, job changes. Not to live in fear, but so you can rest easier knowing you're prepared.

Your money should now work harder than you ever did at six a.m., making breakfasts, packing bags, and coordinating chaos. It should give you choices. It should let you say "yes" to what excites you and "no" to what drains you.

Start small. Open a Freedom Fund account today. Automate ten percent savings this week. Choose one new way to earn or save by the end of the month. You don't need revolution – just consistent steps toward independence.

Because in the end, it's not about being "rich." It's about being free enough to choose. To choose the work you love, the people you spend time with, and the way you spend your days. That freedom is priceless.

Money Power Moves

Exercise 1: "Money Map"

Print out your last month's bank statement (yes, the scary one) or open your app. Highlight three colors: one for needs, one for wants, and one for the future. Then categorize every expense using the 50/30/20 rule[17]. The point isn't to feel guilty about the takeout sushi – it's to see where your money goes. Sometimes, just realizing that "emergency Amazon orders" ate more than your rent is enough to flip the switch.

Exercise 2: "Freedom Fund Kickstart"

Open a separate account–today, not "someday." Please set up an automatic transfer of at least 10% of your income straight into it. Don't wait for a "better month." Don't negotiate with yourself. Treat it like another bill, except this one is paid to the future you. Call it your Freedom Fund, not "savings." Every time you look at the growing balance, remind yourself: this money is not for cleats, braces, or phone repairs. For you, your dreams, your plan B, C, or Z.

Exercise 3: "Skills to Cash"

Make a list of ten things you've done for free as a mom that could make money. Did you coordinate birthday parties like a pro? That's event planning. Did you spend years tutoring your kids in math? That's teaching. Did you manage everyone's schedules and crises? That's project management. Circle two skills that excite you the most and brainstorm how to turn them into a side hustle—freelancing, consulting, or selling online. You don't need to build an empire overnight. You need proof that what you already know has value beyond your personal experience.

PART III

Flying Solo (And Loving It)

Chapter 12

The Relationship Reckoning — Midlife Marriage Renovation Or Demolition: Your Choice, Your Terms

> *The meeting of two personalities is like the contact of two chemical substances: if there is any reaction, both are transformed.*
>
> Carl Jung

Last night you stood in the bathroom brushing your teeth side by side, like every evening for the past twenty years: same routine, same spots at the two sinks, same rhythm of getting ready for bed. But suddenly something shifted. In the mirror, you caught each other's eyes, and for a moment, you looked at each other like strangers. Who is this woman? Who is this man? And where did this weird feeling come from, like you're living with a roommate instead of a husband?

For the first time in years, the house wasn't filled with sounds of music from teenagers' rooms, shouts about missing socks, or phones ringing with questions about who's where. There was just silence. And in that silence, you realized something terrifying: for years, you'd functioned mainly as a parenting tag team, and you'd forgotten how to be a couple.

All your conversations for months had revolved around kid logistics. "Remember, Anna has the dentist tomorrow." "Tom needs money for the field trip." "Who's picking up Katie from practice?" Even your rare dinner conversations were about their plans, their problems, their futures. When was the last time you talked about your plans as a couple?

Last Saturday, you went to the mall together, for the first time in months, without a specific mission to buy something for one of the kids. And you stood in the middle of the main corridor, not knowing where to go. Where did that couple, before kids, used to go? What did they do for fun? What hobbies did you have together? You couldn't remember. In the car on the way home, there was awkward silence, so you turned on the radio, as if music could cover up the fact that you'd become strangers who share an address and common memories but no longer have common topics.

And now, with the house empty, you're alone with each other for the first time in decades, and you're facing one of the most challenging questions of your life: who are we to each other without kids?

Every couple asks themselves this question after the empty nest, but few dare to say it out loud. Because the answer might be too painful, you might discover that for all these years, you were great colleagues in the family business, but you forgot how to be lovers. You might find out that you focused so intensely on raising children that you stopped growing as a couple.

Or (and this is equally terrifying) you might discover that you do like each other, but you can't remember how.

Last week, you tried to organize a romantic evening. You made reservations at that elegant restaurant downtown, the one you hadn't been to in years because the kids preferred pizza or burgers. You dressed up like for a real date, not like for a quick dinner between dropping one kid off at practice and picking up another from tutoring. But sitting across from each other by candlelight, you realized you didn't know what to talk about without kids as a safe topic.

You tried to remember what used to connect you. Movies? But his taste in films hasn't changed in twenty years, while yours has evolved in directions he doesn't understand. Travel? But all your trips together for years have been family vacations, where the main criteria were pool access and proximity to kid-friendly attractions, not whether the place inspired you as a couple of adults. After two hours, you came home earlier than planned, pretending you were tired.

A week later, your sister asked how the romantic evening went, and you were at a loss for words. Was it nice? Did you feel close? Was there anything there that reminded you of the old chemistry? Or did you sit across from each other like two people who'd accidentally been assigned to the same table at a restaurant?

The problem is you became experts on someone else's life and forgot your own. You know every detail of your teenager's social life, but you don't know who your husband has lunch with at work. You remember all the important dates related to the kids, but you can't remember when you last celebrated something as a couple, not as a family. When did he last buy you flowers, not on Mother's Day, but just because he thought of you as the woman he loves?

When did he last ask about your dreams that had nothing to do with a better future for the kids? When did he last tell you about something that fascinates him beyond work and parenting? When did you last plan something together that didn't need to be approved by the family committee and adapted to everyone's schedules?

And now, in the silence of the empty house, you're getting the most critical test of your marriage. It could be either the most beautiful gift or the worst nightmare, depending on what lies beneath the layers of parenting routine.

Some couples discover that underneath, they're still best friends. That through all those years of chaos and exhaustion, they still like each other, they just forgot how to express it. That's when they stop being just mom and dad, they remember how to be the woman and man who once chose each other out of millions of other people in the world. These lucky couples, after a few months of awkwardness, start laughing together like teenagers, rediscovering each other. They plan trips to places they'd dreamed about but put off for "when the kids are older." They learn to make love again in silence, without fear that someone will knock on the bedroom door.

But other couples discover something much more complex: that somewhere along the way, they stopped being a couple and became just roommates sharing chores and the electric bill. It happened gradually and imperceptibly, like coastal erosion. It may have started in the first year of parenthood when you were so exhausted that romance seemed like a luxury you couldn't afford. Every free moment during the years with small children went to recovering energy, not building intimacy, which may have deepened the problem. Perhaps it was finalized during the teenage years, when all your emotional energy went to managing their dramas and making sure they didn't do anything you'd regret for the rest of your life.

And now that all the chaos is over, you look at the man washing dishes next to you and ask yourself a question that scares you more than any teenage rebellion: "Do I still love you?"

It isn't an easy question to answer, because love after twenty years of marriage isn't the same as it was at the beginning. It's not butterflies in your stomach or sleepless nights spent talking until dawn. It's something more profound, but also more complicated. It's gratitude that he was there during all the crises, not just the big ones, but the daily ones too, when kids were sick, when you had a bad day at work, when your father died. It's admiration for how he handled the pressure of being a father, even when he had no idea what he was doing. It's the memory of thousands of small gestures - how he brought you coffee when you were sick, how he stayed home with the kids so you could go out with friends, how he never complained when you had to get up at night with a sick child.

But is that love, or just deep friendship and mutual respect for surviving the hardest years of life together?

And is that enough for the next twenty or thirty years?

Some women discover the answer is "no." Over the years, they've changed so drastically that they no longer fit their marriage like a hand in a glove they've worn for twenty years. That they've become different people from the ones who got married, while their husbands stayed the same, trapped in a time capsule from their twenties or thirties. Or the reverse: that their husbands changed in directions they don't like, while they tried to stay the same to maintain stability and family harmony.

Perhaps the most painful discovery of the empty nest is realizing that a marriage that worked perfectly as a framework for raising children completely fails as a space for two adults who want to grow, explore, and dream about things bigger than a college fund for the kids.

I met Barbara at a workshop for women over fifty. She came there two months after her youngest child left for college. During the first meeting, she cried while telling us how, after twenty-three years of marriage, she discovered she had nothing to talk about with her husband. "We sit at breakfast and we're silent," she said. "We don't fight, there's no anger between us. There's just nothing." Six months later, Barbara decided on a separation. Not because she didn't like him. Because she realized she liked him the way you want a good neighbor or work colleague, but that's not enough for the rest of your life.

And then there's Linda, who chose a completely different path. When her kids left, she and her husband also found themselves in the same situation: they didn't know how to be together without kids as the central topic. Instead of giving up, they decided to treat it like an adventure. They signed up for a dance class they'd never tried, planned little weekend trips to places that had always intrigued them but weren't exactly "family-friendly," and bought bikes to explore local trails together. Today, three years later, Linda says she loves her husband more than ever, but in a completely different way, as a partner in life's adventure, not just as a co-parent.

And then there's a third group of women: those who are already single, whether through divorce in earlier years,

death of a partner, or by choice. For them, an empty nest is a double challenge. Not only do they stop being full-time moms, but they also have to learn again who they are as single women over fifty in a world that often treats single women over fifty as invisible or somehow deficient. **Anna has been single by choice for ten years now.** When her kids were small, she divorced her husband, who, as she says, "was a good man but a bad husband for me."

During the last few years of intensive single parenting, she didn't have time or energy to think about romantic relationships. But now that her child is in college, she suddenly has mental and time space to wonder: does she want someone in her life again?

"For months I couldn't decide," Anna tells me. "On one hand, I'm sometimes lonely. On the other hand, for the first time in twenty years, no one expects me to be available at all hours of the day and night. No one leaves dirty socks on the floor. No one complains about what I cook for dinner. I'm free to watch whatever I want on TV, sleep in the middle of the bed, and leave the house without explaining where I'm going. After a year of reflection, Anna decided to try dating, but on her terms. "If I find someone who adds to my life instead of subtracting from it, great. If not, I'm okay with that too."

And here's a truth that few people say out loud: dating after fifty is an entirely different game than dating when you're young. You're not looking for someone to build a life from scratch with, plan children, and coordinate careers. You're looking for someone who fits into the life you've already shaped according to your preferences and needs. Someone who understands that you have adult children, a complicated past, established routines, non-negotiable preferences, that your energy isn't unlimited, and you won't pretend to be someone else for the sake of a relationship.

But paradoxically, this can also be more honest and ultimately satisfying than dating in your youth because you know what you want. You know what you absolutely can't tolerate based on decades of life experience. You don't have to pretend you're flexible on things that fundamentally matter to you. You can be authentically yourself from the first date, because life has taught you that pretending to be someone else is not only exhausting but ultimately doomed to failure.

The problem is that "yourself" for the first time in twenty years means "yourself without kids as the main source of conversation topics and personal identity." Who are you on a date when you can't spend the first hour talking about your children, their achievements, their struggles, their bright futures? What do you talk about with a strange man when the central part of your identity for years was motherhood?

Katie, forty-nine, describes her first date after divorce as an "absolute disaster." "I sat across from this nice man, and after ten minutes of small talk, I didn't know what to say. My entire adult life had revolved around kids. When I tried to talk about myself, everything somehow came back to them. And when I tried not to talk about the kids, I felt like someone who'd lost their memory and couldn't remember who they were." But Katie didn't give up. The next day, she wrote a list of things about herself that had nothing to do with motherhood. At first, she had only five items. Today, a year later, she is thirty and is in a happy relationship with a man who, as she says, "fell in love with me as a woman, not as an experienced mother."

It can be a terrifying discovery: that you don't remember how to flirt as a woman, not as a mother. How to be mysterious and intriguing instead of just reliable and nurturing. How to present yourself as an interesting person in your own right, not just as someone with extensive parenting wisdom.

But it can also be incredibly liberating because you can flirt differently after fifty. You can be confident in a way that wasn't possible in youth, when you were full of insecurities and desperate for approval. You can know what you want from a relationship and not be afraid to articulate it from the very beginning. You can have standards based on life experience, not on romantic fantasies or social expectations.

Regardless of whether you're trying to rebuild an old marriage, looking for new love, or learning to be happy alone, one thing is sure: your approach to relationships must fundamentally change.

Because you're not the same woman who entered your previous serious relationship, you're wiser, stronger, and more aware of your own needs and limitations. You have less time for nonsense and emotional games, but more capacity for real depth and authenticity. You have less tolerance for relationships that don't serve you, but more appreciation for connections that truly enrich your life.

You no longer have to make the compromises you made in youth out of desperation, fear of loneliness, or social pressure. You can choose from a position of strength, not weakness. You can say no to relationships that diminish you and yes only to those that celebrate who you are, not who you think you should be.

Your empty nest isn't just the end of intensive motherhood. It's also the beginning of the most authentic chapter in your romantic history. Whether it's a continuation of an old story with renewed energy, a completely new adventure, or a peaceful, fulfilling single life - the choice is yours in a way that wasn't available for decades.

But one thing is sure: you deserve love that celebrates you as a complete, complex human being, not just as a devoted mother. You deserve a relationship that enhances who you are becoming, not just accommodates who you used to be.

Time for a reckoning with love.
What story do you want to write in this next chapter?

RELATIONSHIP RECKONING: Exercises

Exercise 1: Relationship Archaeology

If you're in a relationship, make two quick lists. First: what you love about your partner as a person (not as a parent). Second: the dreams you once shared as a couple before kids. Which dreams still matter? Which ones could you bring back to life together?

Exercise 2: The Conversation Experiment

Set aside 30–45 minutes for a conversation with your partner (or, if single, with yourself in a journal)–the only rule: no talking about kids. Talk about anything else. If the silence feels awkward, notice that too – it tells you something about where your relationship stands.

Exercise 3: Letter from Your Future Self

Write a letter to yourself as if you were 75 years old, looking back on your love life in your sixties and seventies. What are you grateful you dared to do? What do you regret not trying? What risks were worth taking?

Exercise 4: Identity Beyond Motherhood

Write a dating profile for who you are right now, no matter your relationship status. One sentence about having kids is allowed. The rest must be about you as an individual. What do you learn about yourself when you write it this way?

Exercise 5: Relationship Compass

Make a list of your non-negotiables in love at this stage of life. What will you no longer tolerate? What needs to be present for a relationship to feel worth your time and energy? Let this list reflect your hard-earned wisdom, not outside expectations.

Chapter 13

Love Without Hovering — Staying Close To Your Grown Kids Without Being The Clingy Mom

> *The days are long, but the years are short. And then suddenly, they're gone.*
>
> Gretchen Rubin

You're standing in the kitchen at eight in the morning and instinctively reach for your phone to text your daughter: "*Remember to take an umbrella, they're forecasting rain.*" Your finger hovers over the screen when you suddenly stop, because your daughter is twenty-two years old, lives three hundred miles away, and can probably check the weather forecast herself. But for twenty years, you reminded her daily about jackets, backpacks, sandwiches, homework–so how do you stop this automatic gesture of care now?

You put the phone back in your pocket, but the anxiety lingers. Your mind is swirling with questions: Is *she eating well? Does she have money for food? Is her roommate distracting her from studying? Is that boy she's dating treating her with respect? Is she happy in this new life she's building without me?*

And suddenly you're hit with a truth that hurts more than any teenage rebellion: your child doesn't need you anymore—at least not in the way you've been required for the past twenty years.

It doesn't mean she doesn't love you; it means you did your job as a mother so well that you've become unnecessary in the daily life of the person you love most in the world.

The paradox of motherhood no one warned you about is this: for eighteen years, your mission was to raise an independent, capable human being. When you succeed, your "reward" is standing on the sidelines, watching them live without you.

Last night you called your son to "just check how he's doing," and after two minutes he said: "*Mom, everything's fine, but I have to go—I'm meeting friends.*" You hung up with a mixture of pride and grief: pride, because you raised someone with a rich social life and healthy boundaries; grief, because you remember when those phone calls lasted hours, when you were his first choice for every problem or joy. Now you're just one of many people in his life. That's how it should be—yet no one told you it would sting this much.

For twenty years, you were the manager of your child's life. You knew their schedule better than your own—tests, practices, social plans, project deadlines. You coordinated, negotiated, solved, and organized. And suddenly you're expected to shift into being... what? An observer? A consultant who gets called only in crises? Someone who waits by the phone, hoping to be remembered on her birthday?

This transition is unlike any other parenting phase. With an infant, you knew dependence would gradually lessen.

With a teenager, you knew rebellion was temporary. But this shift is permanent. Your child won't go back to needing you in the same way. The new reality for the rest of your life is loving from a distance.

Step One: From Surveillance to Staying in Touch

The first step is recognizing the difference between staying in touch and conducting surveillance. Staying in touch means showing genuine interest, respecting privacy, and listening without rushing to give advice. Surveillance means bombarding with questions, expecting daily reports, and demanding access to every detail of their life.

Ask yourself: when you say "*How are you?*" are you really listening, or already preparing advice? When they share a struggle, are you present—or already brainstorming solutions? When they don't reply to a message for two days, do you assume they're busy, or do you imagine worst-case scenarios and start calling their friends?

Step Two: Quality Over Quantity

Your adult child likely prefers one meaningful conversation a week over seven superficial check-ins. Before you send that text, ask: *Is this valuable for them, or just comforting for me?* Learn to filter.

Timing matters too: do you call when it's convenient for you, or when it might be for them? Do you accept that sometimes they won't pick up, not because they don't love you, but because adults need space?

Step Three: Respect Their Privacy

The hardest part is respecting their privacy. You no longer have a right to know every detail—what they earn, who they date, what they eat, why they didn't pick up last night. They may choose to share, but it's not an entitlement anymore.

For years, you knew everything–their friends, their problems, their fears. Now, most of their life happens without you. It's normal, healthy, and appropriate. But for someone who was the center of their universe, it can feel like heartbreak.

Instead of interrogating, shift to open-ended curiosity. Ask "*How was your day?*" instead of "*Did you eat lunch?*"; "*How are things at work?*" instead of "*Is your boss still annoying you?*"; "*I'm happy to hear your voice*" instead of "*Why didn't you text me back?*"

Step Four: Respect Their Choices

Your adult child may choose a partner, career, or lifestyle you dislike. They may live in a city far from you or make financial decisions that scare you. You're allowed opinions–but unless asked, keep them to yourself.

Instead of "*If I were you...*" practice saying: "*If you want to talk, I'm here.*" Or ask: "*Do you want me to listen, or do you want advice?*" And then honor the answer, even if it's just "listen."

Step Five: Build Flexible Traditions

Old traditions worked when your kids lived under your roof. Now they have their partners, friends, commitments. It might mean celebrating Christmas in January, choosing shorter but more frequent visits, or accepting that you won't always be the priority.

It may mcan making space for new faces–partners, in-laws, chosen family. Hard as it is, respecting their importance is part of respecting your adult child's independence.

Step Six: Reframe Independence as Success

When your child handles something on their own, it's not rejection–it's proof you did your job. When they manage finances or relationships independently, celebrate: they've internalized what you taught.

Shift your perspective from "*They don't need me anymore*" to "*I raised them so well that they can handle life on their own.*" That's not loss–it's legacy.

Step Seven: Become a Cheerleader, Not a Manager

You're no longer the organizer of their life. Your role is to encourage, to celebrate, to listen. Offer support when asked–not because you sense they "might need it."

Replace answers with questions, solutions with listening. Trust their ability to navigate life, and trust they'll reach out when they genuinely need you.

Step Eight: Rediscover Yourself

The most vital step: rebuild an identity beyond motherhood. What are your passions, goals, hobbies, and friendships? When you live a whole, vibrant life, your children don't visit out of guilt–they see because you're engaging, inspiring, and enjoyable to be with.

The goal isn't becoming less important, but important in a new way. You're no longer essential for daily survival–but you can be necessary for emotional depth, for wisdom, for unconditional love.

Remember when you let go of your child's hand so they could take their first steps? You felt pride, fear, and overwhelming love. That's what this stage is: letting go again. But now it's permanent. Your role evolves–not into absence, but into something more profound.

Done right, you don't just gain an adult child. You gain an adult friend. One who calls because they *want* to, not out of obligation. One who shares their triumphs because they value your perspective, not because they fear disappointing you.

And that's a love richer, freer, and more meaningful than any you've known before: a love based on choice, not dependency.

LOVE WITHOUT HOVERING: Exercises

1. Communication Audit

For a week, track every interaction with your adult child. Label each: necessary information, worry-driven check-in, or sharing your loneliness. Notice which dominates, and ask if the balance reflects their needs or yours.

2. The 24-Hour Rule

Before calling or texting, wait 24 hours. Ask: *Is this valuable for them—or just soothing for me?* If it's for you, find another outlet (friend, journal, therapist).

3. Boundary Respect Practice

When your child says "*I can't talk now*" *or* "*I don't want to discuss this*", respond with complete respect, not defensiveness. Notice how it changes the interaction.

4. Your Life Beyond Them

Write down three goals for the next six months that have nothing to do with your children—a new hobby, travel, friendships, or learning. Start one now.

5. Love Letter to the Future

Write a letter to yourself describing the relationship you want with your adult child in five years. What kind of mother do you want to be? What role do you want in their life? Use it as a compass for your daily choices in communication.

Chapter 14

Friends Who See You, Not Your Carpool Schedule — Building A Midlife Tribe That Gets You

> *Friendship is the only cement that will ever hold the world together.*
>
> Woodrow Wilson

You're in the grocery store checkout line when you spot Agatha, the woman who once spent eight years helping you coordinate class trips, collect money for teacher gifts, and manage endless email threads about cupcakes for the fundraiser. Back then, ten minutes together was enough to cover everything: how the kids were doing in school, who was friends with whom, who was struggling with math, and which after-school activities overlapped.

Now you stand face to face, and suddenly you realize you have no idea what to talk about. The kids are in college, scattered across different cities: no more carpooling, no games requiring organized cheering, no teenage drama to analyze. After a few minutes of small talk about the weather and grocery prices, you part ways with the unsettling feeling that you just lost a friend you'd spent hundreds of hours with, but never truly knew.

And a question lingers: *do I have real friends?*

For years, you believed you did. Your phone buzzed constantly with messages from other moms about homework, playdates, and permission slips. You spent afternoons in school parking lots talking with other parents. You went to meetings, organized baby showers, and joined book clubs, though the books were often just an excuse to talk about the kids.

But once the kids are gone, many of those relationships fade. They weren't built on genuine connection, but on logistics. Those women knew you as "Tom's mom" or "the one who organizes carpools." But who are you outside of that role?

One evening, scrolling through your phone, you notice you have two hundred contacts. But when you ask yourself, *Who could I call about a personal problem that has nothing to do with my kids?* The list shrinks to three people. And even with them, you realize you haven't shared anything deeply personal in months.

That's one of the surprising realities of empty nest life: social isolation can exist even in the middle of what once looked like a busy social calendar. For years, you were surrounded by people, but most of those interactions were transactional. "Can you pick up Katie if I grab Tom?" "Remember the meeting with the teacher tomorrow?" "Did you hear Anna got into college?" Applicable exchanges, yes. But how often did someone ask, "*How are you doing?*"

For twenty years, your social identity was shaped by your children. Invitations came because your kids were friends. Conversations flowed because you were all juggling parenting. The common denominator was strong. But what happens when it disappears?

Last Saturday, you went to a downtown book fair, your first event in years that wasn't tied to school or family. While flipping through a biography of Marie Curie, a woman your age stopped beside you and said, "Fascinating woman, isn't she? I always wonder what it was like being a pioneer in a man's world." Within minutes, you were deep in conversation, not about children but about ambition, resilience, and what it means to be a woman breaking ground. After an hour, you walked away energized, exchanging phone numbers not because your kids might become friends but because *you* wanted to continue.

That same week, you discovered another possibility. On your evening walks, you noticed a woman taking the same route. After weeks of silent nods, one evening you stopped at the same bench. "Beautiful night," she said. "Yes," you replied, "I finally have time for myself." She laughed, "My kids just flew the coop, too." And there it was—an hour-long conversation about identity, freedom, and rediscovering who you were before motherhood. No logistics, no kid drama. Just two women walking into a new stage of life, side by side.

Making friends in this season is an entirely different skill from "mom friendships." With mom friends, your children are provided with an automatic bond and endless material to discuss. With new friendships, it's about *liking each other as people.* It takes more vulnerability. You have to reveal opinions, passions, quirks, sometimes silly, sometimes serious. You risk rejection, not because your kids don't get along, but because you might not click as individuals.

Your colleague Eva once told you about her book club: "At first we read parenting books," she laughed, "but soon realized our best discussions came from novels, history, and philosophy. That's when we stopped being 'moms reading together' and became women pushing each other's thinking." Some members left when they only wanted to talk about kids, but the rest grew into her closest circle. Friends who know her politics, her fears, her ambitions. *Real friends, not parenting acquaintances.*

That's the heart of post-empty nest friendship: finding people who connect with you for who you are now, not who you were in the school years. But that also means knowing yourself again. What fascinates you? What makes you laugh? What do you want to learn? For years, you developed your children's interests, often neglecting your own. Now, the challenge and the gift are rediscovering them.

Two months ago, you went to an art gallery opening, nervous and unsure. You knew nothing about art and worried about not fitting in. But you found others who felt the same, women curious and open, willing to explore. Now you meet monthly, discussing exhibitions, yes, but also politics, books, and dreams. You didn't become art experts. You became women who support each other in exploring life.

That's the difference between old friendships and new ones. The old were anchored in shared responsibility. The latest are rooted in shared curiosity. But building them takes time. Not everyone you meet will click. Some women stay stuck in parenting mode. Some will be in different life stages. Some won't fit. And that's okay—better two authentic friendships than twenty shallow ones built on convenience.

To find your people, you'll need to step outside old comfort zones. Attend events that genuinely interest you. Try activities you always postponed. Say yes to invitations, even if you feel awkward. Approach women with curiosity, not just as fellow mothers but as full individuals.

And most importantly, be patient with yourself. Your friendship muscles may feel rusty after years of mom-mode connections. You might feel hesitant at first. That's normal. The right people will value your honesty, your humor, your curiosity, and your openness to growth.

Your new friendships can become some of the most meaningful relationships of your life. They won't be based on convenience but on mutual interest and authenticity.

They'll celebrate who you are becoming, not just who you were.

It's time to find your tribe: women who see you as a whole, fascinating person who once raised children, but who is so much more than that.

FRIENDSHIP & CONNECTION: Exercises

Exercise 1: Friendship Map

Look through your contact list and notice the roles people play in your life. Who are your genuine friends, the ones you can talk to about anything? Who are mostly "mom friends," with bonds that existed mainly through the kids? Who are acquaintances or professional contacts? Notice where you feel abundance and where you might want to give or receive more attention.

Exercise 2: Interest Inventory

Make a list of things that fascinate you outside of parenting. Include hobbies you once loved but set aside, as well as new interests you've always wanted to explore. This list becomes a roadmap for connecting with like-minded people. As an extra step, circle one item and commit to trying it within the week.

Exercise 3: Conversation Experiment

For the next seven days, challenge yourself in conversations to avoid mentioning children right away. Let the discussion wander elsewhere first. Notice which topics make you feel most alive and how others respond when you share them.

Exercise 4: Curiosity Challenge

Pick one activity linked to something you've always been curious about but never tried. It could be visiting an art gallery, joining a walking group, seeing a foreign film, or attending a local lecture. Show up with curiosity, not pressure. The goal is to enjoy the experience, not to "find friends" immediately.

Exercise 5: Authentic Self Check

Before your next social event, pause and ask yourself: *How do I want to show up tonight?* Not as the "perfect mom" version or the "impressive professional," but as the version of you that feels genuine, curious, and present. Then notice how people respond when you show up authentically.

Chapter 15

The Holidays Are Yours Now — Creating Joyful Traditions That Don't Require Therapy

> *Traditions are the guideposts driven deep in our subconscious minds. The most powerful ones are those we are not even aware we have.*
>
> Ellen Goodman

It's the first Saturday in November. You're flipping through your calendar when it hits you: Christmas is only six weeks away. For the first time in twenty-five years, you don't know if you'll be cooking for four, two, or maybe just yourself. Your husband might spend it with his sister. Your kids have their plans, partners, and cities.

For decades, the holidays were a well-oiled machine. You knew exactly what to prepare, who would be at the table, which dishes everyone expected, which gifts would delight, and which would disappoint. By early December, the house smelled of gingerbread, the fridge was full of prepped dishes, and you were the conductor of a holiday orchestra.

But suddenly, the script is gone. Last year, your son called to say he was spending Christmas with Jenny's parents in Seattle. Your daughter texted that she had picked up an extra hospital shift in Denver and would stay there. Just like that, you were facing the first holidays that wouldn't resemble the last twenty.

The first reaction was grief, a hollow sadness that caught you off guard. Sitting in the same kitchen where you had planned every holiday, it felt as if you were excluded from your celebration. How could the children, for whom you created magic, now treat it as optional? Were all those late nights baking cookies, hunting for presents, and decorating until your hands ached meaningless?

Yet once the grief softened, another thought appeared: for the first time in decades, you can spend the holidays in a way that reflects what you want.

After so many years of organizing for others, you might not even know what your dream holidays look like. Would a simpler meal feel just as festive as a turkey with ten side dishes? Does the tree need to reach the ceiling, or would a smaller version be enough? Do you want to recreate the picture-perfect holiday, or try something new, like French wine and cheese or Italian prosecco and panettone?

The first Christmas without children can feel like a loss. It can also be the beginning of holidays that feel authentic, where your choices matter more than obligations.

Creating new traditions doesn't erase the old ones. It reshapes them to fit the life you live now. A dinner for two instead of twelve. A single meaningful gift for yourself instead of dozens of obligatory ones. One cozy room decorated for comfort instead of turning the entire house into a magazine spread.

New traditions can also be adventurous. It could be yoga on Christmas morning, a marathon of classic movies with hot chocolate, volunteering at a shelter, or finally traveling instead of staying home. For years, home was the center of your children's world. Now that they are building their own, you can decide where you want to wake up on Christmas morning, whether in the mountains, in New York, or on a quiet beach.

Redefining holidays does not mean losing touch with your children. It means connecting differently. A brunch on December 27th instead of a stressful dinner on the 24th. Shopping together online while on a video call. We are watching the same movie at the same time in different cities and sharing reactions live.

Many of your friends and neighbors are navigating the same stage. Celebrating with girlfriends, couples your age, or chosen family can be just as meaningful. Sometimes it feels even more so, because it is created intentionally rather than out of duty.

The first year may feel raw and heavy. The second year might be about experimenting with smaller gatherings or trips. By the third or fourth year, many women realize they are not longing for the old holidays but looking forward to the new ones.

Children may resist at first. For them, traditions symbolized stability. They may be upset, wondering why everything must change. Over time, when they see you more relaxed and genuinely enjoying the season, they will begin to understand. Some may even look to you as an example when shaping their traditions.

Old traditions served your old life, when children needed magic, structure, and predictability. Now you need something different, holidays that reflect who you have become.

When you stop creating holidays only for others, you finally get to experience them yourself. Smaller gatherings bring deeper conversations. Less cooking leaves more time for what you love. Spending less on obligatory gifts makes space for something meaningful.

The holidays may not look like they used to, but they can feel more real, more peaceful, and in their way, more magical than ever.

HOLIDAY TRANSFORMATION: Exercises

Exercise 1: Holiday Reality Check

Think back to the last three to five holiday seasons. When did you genuinely feel joy, and when did you want to say, "never again"? Make two lists: what gave you energy and what drained it. It will show you which rules are worth keeping and which you can safely let go of.

Guiding questions:

Which moments felt light and fun?

Which ones left you exhausted or resentful?

If you could skip one tradition forever, what would it be?

Exercise 2: Your Holiday, Your Rules

Picture a holiday where no one expects anything from you. Where would you be? What would you eat? Who would you spend it with? What would the morning look like? Write it in detail. This vision can become a map for real change.

Guiding questions:
What would your ideal holiday morning look like?

Who do you genuinely want to share it with?

What foods, sounds, or activities would make it feel special?

Exercise 3: One Change Test

Pick one thing to do differently this year. Bake only the dessert you love instead of three. Swap the stressful gift exchange for drawing names. Take an afternoon walk instead of rushing through errands. A small change will remind you how much freedom you have.

Guiding questions:

What part of the holidays stresses you out the most?

What is one realistic change that would make it lighter?

How will you remind yourself that it is okay to break old rules?

Exercise 4: Letter to December-You

Write a letter to yourself a year from now: how do you want to feel once the holidays are over? What mattered most? What felt like wasted effort? What do you hope you'll remember? Use it as a guide for the years ahead.

Guiding questions:
What emotions do you want to feel at the end of the season?

What memory do you want to create for yourself?

What do you want to avoid repeating?

Exercise 5: New Tradition Tryout

Create one new tradition for yourself, or for you and a partner or friend. It could be a morning walk on Christmas Day, rewatching the same movie each year, or a short trip. Ask yourself why it matters, and commit to trying it.

Guiding questions:
What small ritual would feel like a treat instead of a chore?

Who, if anyone, do you want to include?

How will you make sure this new tradition happens?

Chapter 16

The Body That Carried Everyone — Midlife Health, Hormones, And Finally Putting Yourself First

> *Self-rejection is the greatest enemy of the spiritual life because it contradicts the sacred voice that calls us the 'Beloved.*
>
> Henri J. M. Nouwen

The grocery store checkout line stretches endlessly. While your teenager argues with the cashier about some energy drink policy, you catch yourself shifting your weight from foot to foot because your lower back is screaming. It's not the first time. You suddenly realize you've been having this same conversation with yourself for three years.

Three years.

The woman behind you rubs her temples, muttering about migraines, and for a second, you want to lean over and say, "Don't wait. Don't do what I did." Somewhere between packing school lunches and scheduling dentist appointments for everyone else, you became a master of medical procrastination. Your body turned into a service vehicle: hands for folding laundry, shoulders for carrying emotional baggage, feet for running forgotten items to school.

But when did you stop being the person who lives inside this body?

The evidence is everywhere: the shoulder pain that began when your youngest was in kindergarten and never left, the digestive issues you promised yourself you'd check "soon" back before the pandemic, the automatic "I'm fine" that spills out whenever someone asks how you are. You've become fluent in postponement. "After soccer season ends." "Once we get through the holidays." "When work calms down." Everyone else's needs carried the label "urgent." Yours were filed under "someday."

The longer it went on, the better you got at ignoring your signals. Now, in the silence of an emptier house, those signals have grown louder. Hot flashes you used to dismiss as stress. Periods that come and go without pattern. Nights when you wake drenched in sweat, heart pounding. Looking at your hands in the mirror and suddenly seeing your mother's. Welcome to menopause, colliding head-on with your empty nest years.

It isn't a coincidence. A body once finely tuned for reproduction and caregiving is undergoing a complete shift. Hormones that shaped your moods, energy, and resilience for decades are dropping fast, precisely at the moment you're redefining who you are without children at home.

And here lies the irony: just when your body demands the most care, you finally have the time and space to give it.

Doctor visits no longer require weeks of negotiation with the family calendar. Routine screenings don't have to be postponed because someone else has a crisis. Food choices can center on what nourishes you, not just what's left on the table. Sleep is no longer dictated by teenage drama or the sound of the garage door at midnight. You now have the freedom to honour your body as a priority, instead of pushing it into the background. It's a moment to reclaim the basics you've set aside.

The mammogram, postponed for three years, can finally be scheduled. Blood work becomes a simple calendar entry, not a mountain of logistics. The colonoscopy you dreaded suddenly feels possible. Even quick checks for blood pressure, cholesterol, and thyroid are non-negotiable foundations for health. Preventive care stops feeling like a luxury and becomes the ground you stand on for the decades ahead.

There's liberation in this shift. You can sit with your doctor without rushing. You can ask questions that used to silence you. You can finally treat symptoms you once dismissed as "normal stress." Yet listening closely can also feel frightening. That persistent knee ache might be arthritis. Mood swings may point to hormones or thyroid changes. Memory lapses could be more than "just stress." With the house quiet, your body's voice is no longer muffled.

The truth is simple: your body at fifty is not your body at thirty. It doesn't bounce back as easily, but it isn't broken either. It has new limits, yes, but also new possibilities. Menopause is not an ending. It's the beginning of a stage in which your body exists for you, not for reproduction or constant caregiving.

That shift requires moving from reactive care to proactive care. Instead of waiting until pain forces you into action, you respond to the earliest signals. Meals are chosen for nourishment, not convenience. Movement stops being punishment and becomes exploration: yoga, swimming, strength training, hiking, dancing. The body you once treated as a workhorse becomes a home worth tending.

Menopause reaches far beyond the physical. Dropping estrogen reshapes mood, memory, stress tolerance, and sleep. Combined with the identity shift of no longer being defined by motherhood, it's no wonder many women feel unmoored. Energy surges one day and vanishes the next. Tears come unexpectedly. Nights stretch on sleepless. Patience wears thin.

And yet, countless women describe this stage as the most powerful of their lives. Post-menopausal women often report a clarity they never had before, a refusal to waste energy on nonsense, a newfound stability that anchors them. Emotional storms give way to confidence. Approval-seeking fades. Choices begin to serve the self.

For the first time since early adulthood, your schedule belongs only to you. No school calendars. No pregnancies to plan around. No endless coordination. Your body belongs to you alone. That realization opens the doorway to profound changes.

Exercise shifts from a frantic ten minutes crammed into a busy day to a lifestyle woven into your rhythm. Cooking transforms into a form of care, not duty. Sleep becomes sacred, supported by a mattress that suits you, blackout curtains, and a calming ritual at night. These choices, once impossible, have now become anchors of daily life.

Most importantly, you begin listening with compassion. No more pushing through exhaustion or silencing pain. You learn which foods lift your energy and which drain it. Medical care is no longer delayed with the excuse "someone else needs me more."

Indulgence has nothing to do with it; caring for your body is survival. Your body carried pregnancies, endured sleepless years, absorbed stress, and kept moving through decades of demands. It deserves respect. With attention, it can astonish you with resilience, strength, and vitality.

Menopause and the empty nest are not a double loss. Together, they can become a doorway to the healthiest, most energized, most confident years of your life. You may discover that your fifties bring more vitality than your forties ever did. You may become more adventurous, more grounded, more alive.

Because for the first time in your adult life, your body no longer belongs to everyone else. It belongs to you.

BODY RECONNECTION: Exercises

Exercise 1: "Daily Body Check-In"

Before you even get out of bed, spend five minutes scanning your body from head to toe. Notice your energy level, any tension, comfort, or overall mood. Jot it down in a notebook each morning for a month. Over time, patterns will appear that reveal what your body needs.

Exercise 2: "Health Priority Reset"

Write down all the health concerns you've been putting off–nagging symptoms, missed appointments, things you keep rationalizing away. Sort them by urgency and commit to booking the top five within the next six weeks. Giving your body attention now is one of the best investments you can make.

Exercise 3: "Movement Discovery"

Pick four completely different activities to try over the next month. Include at least one you've always been curious about but never dared to do. It could be dance, martial arts, swimming, hiking, cycling–whatever sparks interest. After each, write a short note about how you felt during and after. The goal isn't perfection, but finding what makes you feel most alive.

Exercise 4: "Intuitive Eating Test"

For two weeks, pause before every meal and ask: *What does my body want right now?* Then do your best to give it exactly that. Pay attention to how different foods influence your energy, mood, and sleep. The goal is to restore confidence in your body's signals instead of relying on strict rules.

Exercise 5: "Self-Care Blueprint"

Design a realistic self-care routine that matches where you are now–not what you think you "should" be doing. Cover the basics: sleep, stress, check-ups, enjoyable movement, nourishing food, emotional balance, and social connection. Start small: add just one element each week. Small, steady steps lead to lasting change, while trying to overhaul everything at once often fails.

Chapter 17

Your Next 30 Years Start Now — Designing A Second Act So Good, Your Kids Will Be Jealous

> *No is a complete sentence.*
> *It does not require justification*
> *or explanation.*
> Anne Lamott

"But you have time now!" You've heard this three times just this week. First, from your sister, who wanted you to take Dad to the doctor. Then, from your daughter, who needed a babysitter. Now, from a friend who assumed you could help her move. And suddenly you realize something frustrating: people see your reclaimed time not as yours, but as theirs to use.

It feels like when your kids moved out, they didn't just take their clothes and books. They also took away your right to your schedule.

Automatically, you find yourself saying "yes, of course" to every request. Even though Wednesday was supposed to be the day you finally went to that yoga class you signed up for a month ago. Even though Saturday was thc day you planned to organize your space to reflect this new stage of life. Even though you have no desire to help someone move who only ever calls when she needs something.

And you realize something important: learning to say "no" may be more complicated than figuring out who you are without kids at home.

Years of mothering trained you to be a "yes" machine. Yes, I can bake for the fundraiser. Yes, I'll drive the kids to practice. Yes, I can stay late at work. Yes, I'll organize the family gathering. Yes, I'll take care of Mom when she's sick. You built your identity by always being the person others could count on.

Now your children no longer need you every day, but suddenly everyone else has moved up in line for your attention.

Your adult daughter calls: "Mom, I know you're not busy with kids anymore, so could you watch Zoey next week?"

Your brother texts: "Can you help Mom with shopping?

You've got more time now." A colleague says, "Since your kids don't live at home anymore, maybe you could stay late and finish this project."

And the worst: "I thought you'd be glad to help now that you're not so busy."

It hits you: while you were preparing emotionally for an empty nest, everyone else was preparing for more access to your time.

One of the most brutal truths about this phase is that even though your children are gone, the line of people wanting your time hasn't gotten shorter. The faces have just changed. And they assume you'll be as available to them as you once were to your kids.

The problem is that for years, you rarely said no. You always managed to squeeze in one more favor. But now the situation is different, even if others don't see it.

At last, you have time that can truly be yours. Time to spend on things that bring you joy, that help you rediscover who you are, that let you build a life beyond motherhood. But other people don't see that as a valuable use of your time. They treat it as something extra, something they can always take.

And here comes the guilt. The same guilt that followed you through motherhood now shows up in a new disguise. You feel selfish when you protect your schedule. You feel like you're letting people down when you say no, even though technically you do have time. You even feel like a bad mother, daughter, sister, or friend for putting your needs first.

But here's the truth: you have the right to your time, even if no one else sees it that way. You have the right to spend Saturday morning with a book instead of cleaning out your sister's garage. You have the right to go to yoga instead of babysitting. You have the right to say no to requests that clash with your plans, even if your plan is "rest."

Learning to say no after years of automatic yes is not just about words. It's a shift in how you see yourself and your rights. For years, your value was measured by how helpful you were. Now you need to know the value of your time and energy.

That means accepting something uncomfortable: you are not responsible for solving everyone's problems. You don't owe anyone an explanation for how you spend your time. Your life belongs to you.

Of course, people won't like this change. They'll be surprised, disappointed, or even accusatory. You'll hear: "I could always count on you." "Family used to be so important to you."

These comments will sting, but they're proof that you're breaking old patterns. People test new boundaries just like children test new rules.

The most important lesson? Your "no" does not need an essay attached. "I can't on Wednesday" is a complete sentence. Not "I can't on Wednesday because I have yoga, and I've been waiting months for this class, and I need it for myself, and I'm sorry, but..." Just: "I can't on Wednesday."

Simple, clear, done.

You can be calm and kind, but also firm. When your daughter says, "I thought you'd be happy to spend more time with Zoey," you can reply: "I love being with her, but I can't be on call. Let's find a time that works for all of us." When a coworker says, "Since you don't have kids at home, you can stay late, right?" you can say: "I have other plans after work. Let's figure out another way."

That's not rude, that's respect.

Part of this shift is also recognizing guilt trips for what they are. "Family must not matter to you anymore." "You've changed." "You never would have said no before." These are not facts. They're manipulations meant to push you back into old habits.

Setting boundaries doesn't make you selfish. It means you finally take yourself seriously. You can still be loving and supportive while being clear about what you will and won't do.

And sometimes, you can offer alternatives. "Not Wednesday, but Friday works." "I can't watch her all weekend, but I can take her to her activity." "I can't stay late tonight, but I can come in early tomorrow." The key is that this is your choice, not your duty. And sometimes "no" means "no."

What may be hardest is dealing with your feelings after saying no. If you've always tied your worth to being needed, the first "no" might feel terrifying. You might wonder if people will still love you if you stop serving them. You might feel anxious, guilty, or even panicked.

But those are old reflexes, not truths. People who genuinely care about you will learn to respect your boundaries. Relationships that existed only because you gave endlessly were never healthy.

You may discover that when you say no to some requests, the times you do say yes feel better, because they come from choice, not obligation. You may also realize that some people disappear when you stop being endlessly available. Painful, yes. But also freeing, because it shows you which relationships were genuine and which were built only on what you could give.

Learning to say no is also learning to say yes to yourself. Every no to someone else is a yes to your priorities, your rest, your passions, your well-being. It may be the first time in your adult life that your needs get to come first. But no one else will protect that for you. You have to do it yourself.

And remember: it gets easier with practice. The first times will be difficult, full of guilt and second-guessing. But with time, it becomes natural. People adjust. And you discover that life with boundaries is more prosperous, freer, and more joyful than life as someone who always says yes.

The art of saying no is the art of loving yourself enough to protect your own life. It's about honoring the value of your time and energy, and building relationships based on mutual respect instead of one-sided giving. And when you stop saying yes to what drains you, you'll have more energy and joy for the things you genuinely want to embrace.

Now ask yourself: what is one request you could say "no" to this week so that you can say a stronger "yes" to yourself?

BOUNDARY-SETTING: Exercises

Exercise 1: "The Guilt Detective"

For two weeks, notice every time guilt shows up when you think about saying no—even if you don't say it. Write down the exact thought: "*She'll think I'm selfish,*" "*What if she never asks me again?*" "*Good mothers don't refuse their kids.*" Then flip each thought into a kinder truth: "*I deserve boundaries,*" "*Real relationships survive honesty,*" "*Respectful mothers also respect themselves.*" Over time, you'll start spotting how often old beliefs—not reality—trigger your guilt.

____

____

____

____

Exercise 2: "No Rehearsal Theatre"

Stand in front of a mirror and practice saying no. Begin with simple scenarios: "No, *I can't bake cookies for the fundraiser.*" Then work up to the tougher ones: "No, *I can't move in to care for Dad.*" Notice your body language. Do your shoulders slump? Do your hands wave around, as if you're trying to soften the blow? Practice saying no with a steady voice, eye contact, and calm posture. Your body needs to believe your boundaries before anyone else will.

Exercise 3: "The Relationship Reality Check"

List the five people who ask you for help the most. For each, ask yourself: Do they show up when you need support? Have you ever asked them for help—and if so, did they deliver? Would they respect a firm no, or would they argue and guilt-trip? When was the last time they reached out to connect? Writing this down can highlight which relationships are mutual and which ones have kept you stuck in the role of constant giver.

Exercise 4: "Time Reclamation Project"

For one week, track precisely how many hours you spend on other people's requests, favors, and "emergencies." Count drive time, prep time, and even recovery time. At the end, total it up. Then ask yourself: "*If I had these hours back, what would I do?*" Learn Italian? Start a book? Visit a museum? Paint? Try one of those things for at least an hour, so the vision becomes real—not just theoretical.

Exercise 5: "Boundary Victory Log"

Keep a log of every boundary win, no matter how small. Write down what you said, how the person reacted, and how you felt afterward. Rate your confidence before and after. Include micro-victories too: not saying yes right away, asking for time to think, or turning down plans that don't excite you. Over time, this log becomes proof that you're getting stronger. Treat it like leveling up in a game–the more you practice, the more natural it gets.

Epilogue

Your Empty Nest Just Got An Upgrade

You are closing this book and perhaps wondering: "What will this look like in a year? In five years? Can I do it?"

The truth is that it will not always feel simple. Not because of age or tiredness, but because choosing what you genuinely want requires a kind of courage no one ever taught you. It is the courage of placing yourself at the center after years of being needed by everyone else.

Six months from now, you might be staring at an application form for a course you have secretly dreamed of taking. Panic will rise: "I don't belong there. Everyone will be younger. What am I even doing at my age?" And then comes the moment of decision. You can close the laptop, or you can take a deep breath and press submit.

That single act will not only enroll you in a class, but it will also announce to yourself that you are stepping into the world as a woman with her ambitions.

On an ordinary Tuesday, someone will ask you for a favor you do not want to do. The reflex to say yes will appear instantly, but this time you will hear yourself respond differently: "I really can't." Their surprise or irritation will be almost visible. For a second, you may feel the urge to explain, but you will stop. The realization that your limits deserve respect will feel unfamiliar at first and then deeply liberating.

A year from now, you may find yourself doing things that today feel out of reach. Perhaps you will be sitting in a café in a city you once only imagined visiting, thinking: "I am here, on my own, and I am not afraid." Perhaps you will be engaged in a conversation about a project that excites you, and you will notice the other person sees you not only as someone's mother but as a woman with ideas. Or perhaps you will be at home in the evening, touched by a quiet sense of peace: "This is my life. I chose it. And I love it."

There will also be more challenging moments. Your daughter might call, exhausted and overwhelmed by work, and every instinct will push you toward fixing things. Instead, you will pause and say: "That sounds tough. What options do you see?" It will hurt not to rush in and solve everything, and at the same time, it will be beautiful, because you will watch her grow strong enough to carry her weight.

There will be days of loneliness that feel deeper than anything you experienced while rushing through errands or sitting in traffic. You will notice how often you used busyness as armor against silence. At first, that quiet may feel unbearable, but with time, you will begin to recognize it as a doorway. Slowly, you will meet yourself there, and you may even start to like the woman you find waiting.

Three years from now, people around you will start to notice. They may whisper, "Something about her feels lighter, more alive." Others will observe: "She carries herself with calm, as if she knows something we do not." What they are sensing is the difference between a life lived out of duty and a life built on conscious choice.

Not everyone will approve. Some will complain that you have changed, longing for the version of you who was always available. You will face the question of whether their discomfort is your responsibility. And the answer will be clear: it does not.

In five years, the life you have been shaping step by step will feel entirely your own. It might include travel, creative projects, or a new vocation. Or it may mean living your days with the freedom and ease you once thought impossible. Whatever form it takes, it will be yours because you chose it deliberately.

What matters most is understanding that change does not arrive through a single dramatic leap. It grows out of many small and consistent acts of courage. Each no that protects your time makes space for a deeper yes to yourself. Each decision to use your energy differently marks another step. And with every step, you move closer to a life that reflects who you truly are.

One morning, you will wake up in that life. It will not be perfect, but it will be real, and real carries more power than any ideal ever could because it belongs to you.

**Now begin creating it,
one brave choice at a time.**

To You

Thank you for arriving here. It means you gave yourself the gift of time, space, and courage to look more deeply into your own life. I know the path through these pages was not always easy. Some words may have stirred old wounds, while others may have opened laughter, relief, or quiet recognition. Every response matters because every response is a sign that you are listening to yourself.

When I began writing this book, I imagined women like you–women who have spent years showing up for everyone else and are now learning how to stand fully present for themselves. If at any moment along the way you discovered a thought that shifted your perspective, or even the tiniest spark of hope, then the journey we shared has already fulfilled its purpose.

I want to remind you that your right to happiness is not something you need to earn, defend, or prove. Each small step you take toward a life that feels authentically yours is not only an act of courage but also a declaration that your story still unfolds, still grows, still matters.

With gratitude and care,

Natalie Huley

Did You Enjoy The Book?

You've reached the end – I truly hope this book gave you something to think about, maybe a smile, or even a fresh perspective.

If you enjoyed it, I'd be so grateful if you could leave a quick review.

It only takes a minute and helps other women discover the support they might be looking for.

Scan the QR code below to go directly to the Amazon review page.

Please text me directly at contact@huleypublishing.com if you feel something is missing or could be improved. Your honest feedback helps me grow and create even better resources for you.

Thank you for being part of this journey!

With gratitude,
Natalie Huley

I ENJOYED

IT COULD BE BETTER...

contact@huleypublishing.com

BONUS

The First 30 Days Of Rediscovery— An Empty Nest Survival Plan

> *A journey of a thousand miles begins with a single step.*
>
> Lao Tzu

(He probably never had teenagers, but the point still stands.)

You've reached the end of this book. Along the way, maybe you underlined a sentence that struck you, perhaps you laughed, maybe you cried. And now, with the final page behind you, the question appears: where do I begin? That is precisely why this roadmap is here.

The 30-day plan will not transform you into an entirely new person overnight, and it won't give you perfect clarity every morning. What it will provide you with is structure at a time when so much of your old structure has disappeared. It offers small, realistic steps that guide you from the fog of "I don't know what to do with myself" toward the steady confidence of "I can see how this might work."

Within these pages, you'll find the first seven days of the plan. Consider it a gentle invitation into rediscovery, with daily prompts and challenges designed to spark reflection and create momentum. If you find yourself enjoying the process, you can continue with the complete 30-day roadmap, which is ready for you to download.

No test, no pressure. The guide is meant to help you begin shaping a life that feels authentic and energizing again.

Remember: even the most minor change counts, and those small victories build more quickly than you might imagine.

So take a breath, turn the page, and step into your next chapter.

Scan me:

WEEK 1
CONSCIOUS AWARENESS

This week is about slowing down enough to hear your voice again. Nothing to fix yet—only noticing what is already there.

DAY 1: The 6 am Test

Challenge: Wake up 30 minutes earlier than usual and pay attention to where your mind naturally wanders in the quiet before the day begins.

Question: What thoughts arise when there are no immediate demands on my attention?

Today's gain: You created space to hear your thoughts without distractions.

DAY 2: The Inspiration Hunt

Challenge: Find one story (online, magazine, or book) about a woman who started something new after 50.

Question: What about her journey resonates with what I am feeling now?

Today's gain: You actively looked for proof that reinvention is possible at your age.

DAY 3: The Curiosity Call

Challenge: Reach out to someone whose life or work intrigues you—even to say, "I've always wondered how you got into that."

Question: What holds me back from expressing genuine curiosity about other people's paths?

Today's gain: You practiced reaching out from a place of authentic interest.

DAY 4: The Expert Encounter

Challenge: Have a conversation with someone who knows more about a subject you're curious about—even something as simple as asking your yoga instructor about their training.

Question: What would I like to understand better, purely for my interest?

Today's gain: You prioritized learning for the sake of curiosity.

If starting a conversation feels overwhelming, try listening to a podcast interview with someone in a field that fascinates you.

DAY 5: The Photo Archaeology

Challenge: Look through old photos and find moments where you appeared genuinely engaged or joyful—not posing for the camera.

Question: What was happening in those moments that I want more of now?

Today's gain: You uncovered authentic moments of joy from your past.

DAY 6: The Learning Budget

Challenge: Research what it would cost to pursue one curiosity you've always had–a class, a workshop, or a new experience.

Question: If money weren't the primary consideration, what would I most want to learn?

Today's gain: You took your interests seriously enough to explore real possibilities.

DAY 7: The Calendar Archaeology

Challenge: Review your calendar and identify which activities energize you and which ones drain you.

Question: What patterns do I notice about when I feel most alive versus most depleted?

Today's gain: You completed your first week of conscious self-observation.

You've just finished your first week of conscious awareness, and that alone is a meaningful step.

Over these seven days, you've slowed down, listened to your thoughts, and started reconnecting with yourself in ways that may have felt long overdue. It is only the beginning of the journey.

If you'd like to keep building on this momentum, scan the QR code below to download the complete 30-day plan.

The following weeks will take you further—helping you grow in confidence, set boundaries with greater ease, and design a future that feels exciting and entirely your own. These first seven days were simply the warm-up.

What comes next is where change begins to take shape.

Scan me:

References

» Camus, Albert. *Return to Tipasa*. In *Lyrical and Critical Essays*, translated by Ellen Conroy Kennedy. New York: Vintage International, 1970.

» Campbell, Joseph. *The Hero with a Thousand Faces*. Princeton, NJ: Princeton University Press, 1949.

» Coelho, Paulo. *The Witch of Portobello*. New York: HarperCollins, 2007.

» Doidge, Norman. *The Brain That Changes Itself: Stories of Personal Triumph from the Frontiers of Brain Science*. New York: Viking, 2007.

» Erikson, Erik H. *Childhood and Society*. New York: W. W. Norton & Company, 1950.

» Fogg, B. J. *Tiny Habits: The Small Changes That Change Everything*. Boston: Houghton Mifflin Harcourt, 2019.

» Goodman, Ellen. At *Large*. New York: Summit Books, 1981.

» Healthdirect Australia. "Understanding Anticipatory Grief." Accessed August 14, 2025. https://www.healthdirect.gov.au/understanding-anticipatory-grief.

» Jung, Carl. *Modern Man in Search of a Soul*. Translated by W. S. Dell and Cary F. Baynes. New York: Harcourt, 1933.

» Kim, Pilyoung, James F. Leckman, Linda C. Mayes, Ruth Feldman, Xian Wang, and James E. Swain. "The Plasticity of Human Maternal Brain: Longitudinal Changes in Brain Anatomy during the Early Postpartum Period." *Behavioral Neuroscience* 124, no. 5 (2010): 695–700.

» Lamott, Anne. *Operating Instructions: A Journal of My Son's First Year.* New York: Anchor Books, 1993.

» Lally, Phillippa, Cornelia H. M. Van Jaarsveld, Henry W. W. Potts, and Jane Wardle. "How Are Habits Formed: Modelling Habit Formation in the Real World." *European Journal of Social Psychology* 40, no. 6 (2010): 998–1009.

» *Lao Tzu. Tao Te Ching.* Translated by D. C. Lau. London: Penguin Classics, 1963.

» Mitchell, Barbara A., and Linda D. Lovegreen. "The Empty Nest Syndrome in Midlife Families: A Multigenerational Perspective." *Canadian Journal on Aging* 28, no. 4 (2009): 475–490.

» Montaigne, Michel de. *The Complete Essays.* Translated by M. A. Screech. London: Penguin, 1991.

» Nouwen, Henri J. M. *Life of the Beloved: Spiritual Living in a Secular World.* New York: Crossroad, 1992.

» Osmosis. "Anhedonia." Accessed August 14, 2025. https://www.osmosis.org/answers/anhedonia.

» Penn, William. *Some Fruits of Solitude in Reflections and Maxims.* Philadelphia: J. Chattin, 1750.

» Rubin, Gretchen. *The Happiness Project.* New York: HarperCollins, 2009.

» Rumi. *The Essential Rumi.* Translated by Coleman Barks. San Francisco: HarperSanFrancisco, 1995.

» Seligman, Martin E. P. "Learned Helplessness." *Annual Review of Medicine* 23 (1972): 407–412.

» Steinem, Gloria. *Revolution from Within: A Book of Self-Esteem.* Boston: Little, Brown and Company, 1992.

» Strayed, Cheryl. *Wild: From Lost to Found on the Pacific Crest Trail.* New York: Alfred A. Knopf, 2012.

» Tedeschi, Richard G., and Lawrence G. Calhoun. "The Posttraumatic Growth Inventory: Measuring the Positive Legacy of Trauma." *Journal of Traumatic Stress* 9, no. 3 (1996): 455–471.

» Walker, Alice. *In Search of Our Mothers' Gardens: Womanist Prose.* San Diego: Harcourt Brace Jovanovich, 1983.

» Wilson, Woodrow. *Address to the Sixty-Fourth Congress.* Washington, DC: Government Printing Office, 1917.

» Woolf, Virginia. *A Room of One's Own.* London: Hogarth Press, 1929.

» Zoe, Rachel. *Style A to Zoe: The Art of Fashion, Beauty, & Everything Glamour.* New York: Grand Central Publishing, 2007.

Printed in Dunstable, United Kingdom

76500194R00103